WHY YOU CAN'T TRUST THE NEWS

Volume 4

Roger Aronoff
Cliff Kincaid

Published by

ACCURACY
in MEDIA

Accuracy in Media, Inc.
4350 East West Highway | Suite 555
Bethesda, MD 20814
www.aim.org

Library of Congress Cataloging-in-Publication Data
(Prepared by The Donohue Group, Inc.)

Lambert, Deborah Ed.
AIM columns compilation - Deborah Lambert, Editor
Project Editor, Mercedes Amaya
Cover design by Louis Tartaglia

Aronoff, Roger
  Why you can't trust the news. Volume 4 / Roger Aronoff,
Cliff Kincaid.

ISBN: 978-0-9895821-0-0

1. Journalism -- Political aspects. 2. Press and politics.
3. Journalism -- Objectivity.

PN4751 .K56 2011
070.4

Printed in the United States of America.

10 9 8 7 6 5 4 3 2 1

First Edition

CONTENTS

FOREWORD

Since the mainstream media appear to spend a good deal of time fretting about diversity in the newsroom, and figuring out how to make America feel guilty, it's a wonder they have any time left to report the facts.

The truth is that factual accuracy ranks quite low on many mainstream journalists' Top Ten list of things to do in order to advance their careers. Telling people what to think has become far more important than teaching them how to think. This is just one of the many reasons that America needs a media watchdog to set the story straight, and provide the public with information they don't receive from the mainstream press.

That's why my father Reed Irvine launched Accuracy in Media over 40 years ago, and why our work is more important than ever today. AIM provides nonpartisan media criticism as a public service, and sets the story straight about issues the media have misreported. This book provides numerous examples of stories that have been misreported or ignored by the mainstream press.

AIM does for the media what they claim to do for every institution other than their own, namely act as an independent watchdog and critic. The Constitutional protection enjoyed by the journalism community demands that the press exercise professional responsibility. Although journalistic societies have codes of ethics that define the boundaries of acceptable conduct, there is no penalty for those who violate those codes.

During the past four decades, AIM has taught an army of citizens how to detect media bias. We have countered false media reports with facts; we have published books, produced award-winning documentaries; confronted the leaders of America's most powerful media corporations at their annual shareholders' meetings; sponsored protests; run nationwide campaigns, and exercised other creative ways to call attention to the problem of media bias.

We will continue to address these problems in our publications, lectures, interviews, films, and media appearances with the goal of raising public awareness and turning the tide. AIM's website at www.aim.org attracts more than a million visitors a year. It offers a wealth of information not available anywhere else. If you would like to become more actively involved with our work, we would welcome your participation.

Don Irvine
Chairman,
Accuracy in Media

CNN'S O'BRIEN URGES OBAMA TO "TRACK" PEOPLE AND FIREARMS

By Cliff Kincaid   December 17, 2012

The Washington Post story, "Media figures on left and right call for new gun-control laws," hailed Soledad O'Brien of CNN for taking a stand in the wake of the Sandy Hook shootings. Pretending to be an intellectual heavyweight on the subject, she declared on the channel that the problem in society is "access to semiautomatic weapons."

O'Brien's embarrassing outburst, which continued for several minutes during an interview with Rep. Mary Bono Mack (R-Calif.), is another indication of why CNN fails to attract many viewers. In its story about the influence of these "prominent media figures," the Post failed to note that there is nothing sinister about "semiautomatic weapons." These are weapons that fire one shot at a time and are used for various purposes, including self-defense.

It appears that O'Brien may have been confusing "semiautomatic weapons" with fully automatic weapons. If she did make this mistake, it would not be unusual for media coverage of a tragedy like this. The liberal media frequently jump to conclusions. In this case, they got the basic facts wrong early in the story, including the name of the shooter.

That the shooter was mentally deranged seems fairly obvious. Rep. Mack's point was that society should address these mental problems. It was not something O'Brien wanted to dwell on.

It is important for people to actually watch or read the exchange O'Brien had with Rep. Mack to understand the liberal fixation on guns rather than on other problems, such as mental illness, or other possible solutions, such as additional security for those at risk of being shot or killed. O'Brien quickly labeled Mack a Republican and tried to put her on the defensive: "You support gun rights in this country. You're a Republican, and I think that's a position very consistent with most Republicans. What does meaningful action that actually stops these kinds of shootings, look like to you?"

With this kind of introduction, O'Brien was making it clear that, in her view, Republicans were partly responsible for the tragedy. She was exploiting the tragedy for political gain, in order to bolster President Obama's call for "meaningful action," whatever that means.

Mack, a rather moderate Republican, replied, in part, that "the question for me is not just gun rights but mental health…And I think if we're going to debate as a country, gun control, we need to debate what we can do better on mental, the mental health system."

Eventually, O'Brien came out with her own dubious "solution." She said, "…I think this conversation at some point has to go to what is the normal amount of guns that people can own and how they're registered and tracked."

What is "normal?" O'Brien didn't say. Who would register and track people with guns? By chance, would it be the Obama Administration?

This is obviously a poorly thought-out "solution" to the violence, typical of a liberal in the media who prefers emotionally-charged rants to rational treatment of serious matters.

CONSERVATIVES IN LIBERAL MEDIA EMBRACE CULTURAL SURRENDER

By Cliff Kincaid   December 10, 2012

As American conservatives contemplate the future of the Republican Party in the face of President Obama's Marxist onslaught, the rapid deterioration of the British Conservative Party stands as proof that the situation could get far worse. British Conservatives lead their government as members of a coalition and are pushing legislation for what they euphemistically dub "Equal Civil Marriage." They think this is the key to being politically relevant and winning elections.

Here in the U.S., former RNC Chairman Ken Mehlman took to the pages of The Wall Street Journal on November 21st to make the "conservative case" for backing gay marriage. But there can be no "conservative case" for gay marriage, unless the term "conservative" is redefined, as the British Conservative leaders are trying to do.

Mehlman, a former lieutenant to Karl Rove, came out of the closet and announced his homosexuality in August of 2010. He has since launched a "Project Right Side" to make the "conservative" case for gay marriage.

Another conservative in the liberal media, George Will, said on ABC's "This Week" show, "the opposition to gay marriage is dying. It's all old people." He had previously endorsed gays in the military and had smeared supporters of the Pentagon's homosexual exclusion policy as unintelligent.

The same "strategy" would also mandate that Republicans should "move on" by abandoning the pro-life cause and opposition to legalization of drugs. That would leave the GOP in the position of running purely on economic issues, in order to draw a contrast with the Democrats. Mitt Romney's stunning defeat is an example of what happens when that strategy is followed.

The American conservative magazine, The American Spectator, which is usually a reliable source of conservative opinion, has published an article suggesting that American conservatives should indeed follow the lead of the British Conservative Party leaders. The author, Robert Taylor, says the British Conservative Party has "stopped trying to turn the clock back to a supposedly golden age of God-fearing, two-parent families" and has become "open, diverse, accepting, individualistic and multi-cultural."

According to this logic, American conservatives should applaud the fact that, on December 1st, the first same-sex couple was "married" in the West Point Cadet Chapel of our nation's military academy.

In Britain, The Sunday Telegraph reports that a survey of British Conservative Party local officials found that 71 percent think the proposal should be abandoned and that the party is losing members as result of the plan.

Christian Concern, a group dedicated to returning the United Kingdom to the Christian faith, says that polling of the general population finds that 18 percent of adults are less likely to vote Conservative as a result of this policy, whereas only seven percent are more likely to do so.

The real lesson from what is happening in Britain is that, if the Republicans go down this road, conservatives will revolt and the GOP will suffer an even more significant decline than we saw on November 6, 2012, when a number of social conservatives sat out the election.

ROMNEY STRATEGIST FAILS TO GRASP MEDIA BIAS

By Cliff Kincaid   November 29, 2012

In his first public criticism of the presidential campaign's media conduct, Mitt Romney's chief strategist meekly suggests reporters "often felt morally conflicted about being critical" of President Obama.

If this is all Stuart Stevens takes away from the campaign coverage, he is woefully ill-informed about media bias. While reporters clearly didn't want to criticize the first black president, Stevens' comment doesn't explain the intensity of attacks on Romney and cover-ups on Obama's behalf.

Stevens wrote his piece defending Romney's campaign for the liberal Washington Post. Jennifer Rubin, a conservative blogger for the paper, points out that Stevens seemed to blame everybody but himself for what went wrong with the campaign.

Stevens was undoubtedly one of those who advised Romney to avoid criticizing the press. We reported on this, noting Romney's comments at the time that he had no plans to challenge media bias and that he would get out his message through other means.

In her criticism of Stevens, Rubin praised another Romney adviser, the lobbyist and former top Republican official Ed Gillespie, as a "class act," when Gillespie had been explicitly quoted as justifying Romney's silence on media bias. Gillespie said the campaign had a "no whining rule" about media coverage.

Gillespie knows better; in his 2009 National Review piece, subtitled, "How the GOP should handle increasingly biased journalists," he wrote that when he joined the Bush

White House in June 2007, "I was still naively hopeful that we could get an honest hearing from the MSM. It did not take long for the scales to fall from my eyes. The national press corps loathed the president—not personally, I don't think, but politically...On issues like the Iraq War, the environment, and life, there was often little distinction between our treatment in liberal blogs and our treatment in major daily newspapers...The lines between news and 'news analysis,' and between 'news analysis' and opinion, have been all but washed away."

Gillespie went on to say there are still "reporters who strive to be fair, report the facts, and avoid commentary," and "...one successful media outlet, the relatively new Politico, seems intent on hiring every 'old school' reporter in Washington."

How wrong Gillespie turned out to be.

Politico is another liberal hired gun that recently hired disgraced journalist David Chalian, who was fired by Yahoo! News for "joking" about Republicans celebrating while blacks were drowning. Several Politico reporters were members of the now-defunct listserv, JournoList, a secret association of several hundred liberal journalists, professors and activists who discussed story ideas and lines of attack on conservatives.

JournoList was started by Ezra Klein while he was blogging for The American Prospect. He later took a position with The Washington Post. Not only is Klein still at the Post, he is said to be in the running to host a new show on MSNBC, the openly pro-Obama cable network.

The title of Gillespie's National Review article was "Media Realism." It looks like he didn't follow his own advice.

SUSAN RICE'S EFFORT TO DEFUSE TALKING-POINTS ISSUE BACKFIRES

By Roger Aronoff   November 28, 2012

Once again, CBS's Sharyl Attkisson is leading the way among mainstream journalists. The winner of this year's Reed Irvine Award for Investigative Reporting is making the obvious point—that the Obama administration can't seem to get its story straight about many aspects of Benghazi-Gate.

The issue at hand is why United Nations Ambassador Susan Rice appeared on five Sunday talk shows on September 16th to explain what happened on September 11th in Benghazi, Libya, with talking points that had been changed to remove their original references to al Qaeda and terrorism. On November 14th, President Obama said she made a "presentation based on the intelligence she had received."

Attkisson pointed out in her article, "Who changed the Benghazi talking points?," that the question arose "when former CIA Director General David Petraeus told members of Congress that his original talking points cleared for public dissemination included the likely involvement by terrorists and an al-Qaeda affiliate. General Petraeus said somebody removed the references before they were used to inform the public."

The first reports had Director of National Intelligence James Clapper making the changes. But later The Cable reported that they were allegedly made by the Office of the Director, but not by the Director himself.

After her Sunday TV appearances, Ambassador Rice met with three Republican senators who had expressed serious concerns, in light of Rice's actions, about her expected appointment as Secretary of State. Acting CIA Director Mike Morell, who accompanied her, told the senators that the FBI had removed the references "to prevent compromising an ongoing criminal investigation."

"But it was just a matter of hours before there was yet another revision," wrote Attkisson. "A CIA official contacted [Sen. Lindsey] Graham and stated that Morell 'misspoke' in the earlier meeting and that it was, in fact, the CIA, not the FBI, that deleted the al Qaeda references."

It is incredible that over two-and-a-half months after the Benghazi terrorist attack, the administration is so caught up in a web of lies that they are still making errors like this.

An article in Wednesday's Washington Post said, "Rice faced some of her harshest critics…about whether she misled Americans…" "Whether she misled" is no longer an issue. The issues are why she misled, who was responsible, and who will be held accountable.

Yet, White House spokesman Jay Carney told reporters on Tuesday, "There are no unanswered questions about Ambassador Rice's appearances on Sunday shows, and the talking points that she used for those appearances that were provided by the intelligence community, those questions have been answered."

Attkisson noted that President Obama likewise indicated on November 14th that "We have provided every bit of information that we have, and we will continue to provide information…We will provide all the information that is available…I will put forward every bit of information that we have." It seems clear the the administration is covering up a scandal.

Hopefully, other reporters will realize the importance of this story and stay on it until the truth is known and people are held accountable.

WHERE THE CONSERVATIVE MEDIA WENT WRONG

By Cliff Kincaid   November 26, 2012

After the election, conservative pundit Ann Coulter tried to rationalize her outspoken support for Mitt Romney in the wake of his stunning defeat. Her most recent column was titled, "Romney was not the problem." "Don't Blame Romney" was written immediately after his defeat and "Romney is What the Country Needs Now" was written immediately before it. She had confidently predicted a Romney victory, tweeting, "I can't see a scenario where Romney wins less than 273 electoral votes."

With stakes so high, it is imperative that if conservative commentators are going to perform a useful function, they should realize where they went wrong and why. Michael Barone, who predicted a Romney landslide, told PJ Media that Romney was "outhustled in a base turnout election" where voter fraud was insignificant.

Steve Baldwin, former Executive Director of the Council for National Policy and a former California state legislator, said the problem all along was "…as any conservative from Massachusetts knew, Romney was a liberal at heart who, as Governor, led the nation in passing three of the left's most sacred issues: Same sex marriage, Cap and Trade, and government control of health care." A significant number of conservatives nationwide clearly did not buy the argument that Romney was legitimately conservative.

One of these issues—same-sex marriage—is worth a detailed examination. After attending Restoration Weekend in West Palm Beach, Florida, Ronald Radosh reported that leading conservative analysts and political leaders have concluded that the Republican Party had to move left on cultural issues.

They need to think harder. First, the movement for gay rights, which is funded by billionaires like George Soros and rich homosexuals, will not accept a truce. Second, in the four states where gay marriage won on the ballot on November 6, 2012, the vote tallies against gay marriage surpassed the vote totals for Romney. In Maryland, Romney was behind the vote for traditional marriage by 12 points. This is telling. It means a certain number of people voted against Obama's position on gay marriage, but they did not vote for Romney. This suggests that Romney failed to rally social conservatives.

Romney's rationale was that the economy would propel him to victory. How many times did we hear "No President since FDR has been re-elected when unemployment is above 8 percent?" Emphasizing his business acumen, Coulter had confidently predicted, "Romney will be the most accomplished incoming president since Dwight Eisenhower."

Bombarded with messages from the Obama campaign and the Soros-funded propaganda machine, including the Super PACs he funded, voters found Romney's private-sector experience on Wall Street and wealth more objectionable than Obama's record as a Marxist president. Of course, Romney never uttered the word "Marxist" or "socialist" when talking about Obama. Romney ran a campaign designed in part to win the votes of those who went for Obama in 2008. It was a disaster in the making that many prominent conservatives in the media did not see coming. Some still do not want to grasp the magnitude of the defeat.

IS PETRAEUS SCANDAL AN OBAMA SCANDAL?

By Roger Aronoff   November 16, 2012

The news media tried to protect the Obama administration from a scandal that gave a black eye to the beginning of the president's second term in office. Scott Wilson of The Washington Post argued that Obama "has been untouched by the unfolding investigation involving former CIA director David Petraeus," a view that belongs on the opinion page under the heading, "wishful thinking."

The stunning news that CIA Director Petraeus had resigned over an affair with his biographer, Paula Broadwell, became the source of numerous theories and psychological questioning of what makes powerful people tick. It was a second shot at what should have been a major Obama administration scandal prior to the 2012 election: the terrorist attacks in Benghazi, Libya on September 11th, 2012.

The Post's Scott Wilson missed the big picture when he claimed the Petraeus "scandal hinges on a personal relationship beyond the White House and has not implicated the president or his closest advisers."

The Post reported that Petraeus had planned to continue in his job as CIA director if his affair with Broadwell was not made public, and he was apparently led to believe it would not go public.

Charles Krauthammer, a columnist for the Post and a Fox News analyst, saw that information as being very revealing: "It meant that he understood that the FBI obviously knew what was going on…and that he understood that his job, his reputation, his legacy, his whole celebrated life was in the hands of the administration, and he expected they would protect him by keeping it quiet."

Krauthammer could only ask, "Was he [Petraeus] influenced by the fact that he knew his fate was held by people within the administration at that time?"

Also, did Attorney General Eric Holder keep the president in the dark about the FBI's knowledge of the scandal nearly six months beforehand? Holder finally offered an explanation publicly almost a week later by saying that he "made the determination as we were going through that there was not a threat to national security." As the Post reported, "Because of that conclusion there was no reason to advise officials outside the department before the investigation was complete."

Rep. Peter King, chairman of the House Homeland Security Committee, said that Petraeus claimed that he had said early on that the attack on the consulate was a result of terrorism. But King seemed puzzled, saying that he remembered Petraeus playing down the role of an al-Qaeda affiliate during his September 13th testimony.

Was Petraeus changing his story and no longer parroting the White House's line?

On that same day, Andrea Mitchell raised the question of Petraeus's responsibility in an interview with Democratic Senator Kent Conrad. "What is David Petraeus's responsibility for this?" asked Mitchell. She went on to ask, "Do you think the agency should bear some responsibility or is this scapegoating after the fact?" Even Sen. Conrad was amused by Mitchell's spin.

This is not what President Obama had in mind for his second term in office.

THE LIBERAL MEDIA ARE MORE POWERFUL THAN EVER

By Cliff Kincaid   November 9, 2012

Before President Obama won reelection, Tucker Carlson and Neil Patel of The Daily Caller contended that bias, dishonesty, and corruption were helping to destroy the liberal media. "The broadcast networks, the big daily newspapers, the newsweeklies—they're done," they said. "It's only a matter of time, and everyone who works there knows it."

Unfortunately, there is no evidence that this is the case. Although liberal news outlets are losing viewers and readers, Obama's victory has actually invigorated them because they correctly predicted the race. They understood the nature of the electorate and how it had shifted in Obama's favor. They achieved something the conservative media were striving for—a measure of credibility. It happened not because of good news reporting, but because of their emphasis on polls and an understanding of how important the progressive infrastructure has become to the Democratic Party machine.

Nate Silver of The New York Times achieved enormous credibility, having correctly predicted Obama's victory and the outcome in 50 out of 50 states. USA Today noted, "Silver had been under fire from Republicans for consistently putting Obama's chance of winning in a range of 60-90 percent."

Bret Baier used his "Winners & Losers" segment on the Fox News Special Report to acknowledge that liberal-leaning presidential election polls came out on top this year. He noted that a Fordham University study "credits the Democratic-leaning Public Policy Polling (PPP) as the most accurate of the survey companies this year." PPP, which also does a poll in partnership with the Daily Kos and the Services Employees International Union (SEIU), came in second.

The Rasmussen Poll, a conservative favorite, was near the bottom of the list of the 28 polling organizations. In fact, Rasmussen had Romney leading Obama 49-48 percent on Election Day.

University of Colorado political science professors Kenneth Bickers and Michael Berry had projected an Electoral College landslide for Romney based on a model using economic data.

"The model was wrong," Bickers is now quoted as saying. Eric Gorski of the Denver Post reported, "Bickers said the Obama campaign managed to neutralize Romney's 'strengths on economic stewardship'—exit polls showed voters held similar views on each candidate's ability to steer the economy—in part by shifting attention to issues such as immigration and women's reproductive rights that play to Obama's strengths."

None of this negates the fact that Carlson and Patel were correct in their analysis of liberal media bias. They wrote, "Not in our lifetimes have so many in the press dropped the pretense of objectivity in order to help a political candidate. The media are rooting for Barack Obama. They're not hiding it…The good news is, it's almost over."

But it's not over. Conservative use of flawed polling data has played into the hands of the liberal media. In order to recapture credibility in covering politics, the conservative media will have to acknowledge not only the bias on the other side, but the bias on their own side.

SHAMEFUL MEDIA COVERAGE OF BENGHAZI SCANDAL AND COVER-UP

By Roger Aronoff   November 6, 2012

Although the mainstream media outdid themselves in manipulating public opinion during the 2012 presidential campaign, the most outrageous act of media malpractice was their coverage of the tragic Benghazi attack that killed Ambassador Chris Stevens and three others, including two former Navy SEALs. From the outset, Obama and others speaking for the administration claimed the attack was the result of a spontaneous demonstration sparked by anger over an anti-Islamic video made in the U.S. And that was just the beginning.

As the story unfolded, we were reminded that there had been a series of violent attacks in Benghazi in April and June of 2012 by so-called "militants," which were carried out on the U.N., the Red Cross, the U.S. consulate, and the British consulate. There had been requests for additional security by Ambassador Stevens and others who worked there, but they were denied. Evidence showed that even though President Obama and his national security team were able to watch part of the September 11th attack in real time, they failed to call in back-up support. Within two hours of being notified that there was an attack under way at the U.S. diplomatic mission in Benghazi, the White House received an email from the State Department stating that a specific terrorist group with ties to al Qaeda had taken credit.

Fox News and, in particular, Jennifer Griffin and Catherine Herridge, have led the way on this important story. The evidence, including classified documents leaked to Fox News, showed that the U.S. Mission in Benghazi had "convened an 'emergency meeting' less than a month before the assault that killed Ambassador Stevens and three other Americans, because Al Qaeda had training camps in Benghazi and the consulate could not defend against a 'coordinated attack.'"

The rest of the media largely stayed away from the story. Although NBC's Brian Williams spent two days with Obama for a long feature story, he asked the president one softball question about Benghazi, which Obama answered with his standard delay-until-after-the-election answer. Williams offered no follow-up.

During a DOD news briefing, Secretary of Defense Leon Panetta explained that the reason no troops were sent in to attempt a rescue was that "The basic principle is that you don't deploy forces into harm's way without knowing what's going on, without having some real-time information about what's taking place."

Maj. Gen. Patrick Brady, U.S. Army (Ret.) wrote in WorldNetDaily, "On its face, that is a remarkable, indeed incomprehensible, change from America's doctrine in past wars. By that standard, there would have been no Normandy or Inchon. In fact, I can't think of a war we fought in which we didn't go into harm's way without real-time information or to save lives—something the president refused to do in Benghazi."

What should have been a full-blown scandal before the election was largely swept under the rug by the mainstream media until the last week or two before voting began. Obama owes a debt of gratitude to his media allies who covered for him in the best way they knew how.

FRANK GAFFNEY: ARE WE BETTER OFF NOW?

By Roger Aronoff   October 18, 2012

During an AIM conference in September 2012, entitled "ObamaNation: A Day of Truth," Frank Gaffney addressed the attendees about "The Muslim Brotherhood in America," during which he explained the extent to which that organization – both directly and through American front groups – has penetrated the highest reaches of our government.

In his speech, excerpts of which you will find below, he talked about whether or not the U.S. was better off today, in terms of foreign affairs and relations with other countries, than we were when President Obama came to power in 2009. His conclusion is that we are not.

Gaffney's wide-ranging experience includes working at the Reagan Defense Department where he was appointed Assistant Secretary of Defense for International Security Policy, and his non-profit national security work. He is the founder and president of the Center for Security Policy, a Washington, D.C. think tank that has focused has focused on the organization, management and direction of public policy coalitions to promote U.S. national security for more than 25 years.

His comments on Iran, Russia and Venezuela are available below:

Frank Gaffney:

> "Iran, of course, is a problem on a myriad of different scores. It is, of course, run by an Islamist regime, albeit of the Shi'ite stripe. It has been engaged in terror; it has, for that matter, been at war with us since 1979. It has been destabilizing

23

its neighborhood and anyplace else it can get its operatives, including now, increasingly, as I'll say in a moment, our own hemisphere. We're learning that it is engaged in cyber warfare against American entities right now, and I suspect that that will kick up more. And, of course, at any given moment we may well see the Strait of Hormuz closed, at least temporarily, with all kinds of repercussions for energy flows and the world economy. Then, as if that weren't enough, there's the nuclear weapons program, which is, I believe, at the cusp of finally realizing the decades-long ambition of the Mullahs to acquire and, perhaps, to use nuclear weapons."

Regarding Russia, Gaffney called the Obama "reset policy" a failure, and said that the "flexibility" Obama promised to Russian Prime Minister Dimitri Medvedev, should he be re-elected, isn't going to be good for this country. He also expressed concern about the "increasing aggressiveness of the Chinese."

On Hugo Chavez and Venezuela:

Frank Gaffney:

"The point of Hugo Chavez is not simply to destroy democracy and any remnant of pro-American sentiment in his own country; he's seeking to do it through the region much more broadly, and has brought to power a number of proxies, in Ecuador, Bolivia, and Nicaragua, and elsewhere for that purpose. He is, in fact, I believe, implementing Fidel Castro's grand design; he long ago ran out of money to pursue it, but Hugo Chavez, with the oil wealth of his country, or at least what used to be the oil wealth of his country, has been able to surmount it."

BIG BIRD IS A DEMOCRAT DUPE

By Cliff Kincaid   October 8, 2012

The George Soros-funded Free Press Action Fund describes itself as "a nonpartisan organization," which "does not support or oppose any candidate for public office." However, at one of the 2012 presidential debates, it announced that the "attack on Big Bird and the Corporation for Public Broadcasting" had "sparked intense reactions from public media fans." Then it said, "The nation is standing with Big Bird. Now it's your turn."

The "attack," coming in the form of Mitt Romney's comments about the need to defund public broadcasting, was based on the recognition that pouring taxpayer money borrowed from China into a U.S. corporation, Sesame Workshop, doesn't make sense.

The controversy not only serves to demonstrate how the "non-profit" entity is making big bucks at the expense of American taxpayers, but how it is working with the Democratic Party, the United Nations and even the Chinese government.

Republicans have long recognized the public broadcasting establishment was a political enemy.

Even before Romney made his comments, the Republican Study Committee (RSC) in the House had proposed eliminating the $445 million annual payment that goes to the Corporation for Public Broadcasting, which finances public TV and radio. The House voted 228 to 192 in 2011 for H.R. 1076 to prohibit federal funding of National Public Radio. The bill died in the Senate. Rep. Doug Lamborn, the sponsor of H.R. 1076, also sponsored H.R. 69, a bill to eliminate all federal funding for the Corporation for Public Broadcasting (CPB).

In response to Romney's pledge to defund public

broadcasting, Lamborn said, "Like Mitt Romney, I like Big Bird. That is not the issue. The governor recognizes the larger problem is out-of-control government spending. I like the governor's test for what programs to keep and what to cut. It's common sense."

On the other side, Democratic Rep. Earl Blumenauer created the Congressional Public Broadcasting Caucus in the 106th Congress to preserve its funding. "Perhaps we need Big Bird to educate Governor Romney about the value of public broadcasting and investing in services for the American public instead of coldly shutting them down," he said in response to Romney's debate comments.

But Sesame Workshop is a rich corporation whose top executives make hundreds of thousands of dollars a year, and the company maintains investments in controversial hedge funds.

Sesame Workshop, which reported revenue of $130,606,413 in 2009, said that 35 percent came from "corporate, foundation and government support." The latter includes the U.S. Agency for International Development, the Department of Education, the Department of Defense, the U.S. Department of State, the U.S. Department of Health and Human Services, and the National Science Foundation (NSF).

Direct government grants amounted to $7,968,918. Its Form 990 reported lobbying expenses of $1 million a year, in order to keep federal dollars flowing.

Senator Jim DeMint (R-SC) pointed out that "From 2003 to 2006, Sesame Street made more than $211 million from toy & consumer product sales," which meant that it could obviously survive without public funding.

Speaking of China, Sesame Workshop not only operates on funds borrowed from China, but it also works directly with the Chinese regime and its communist army.

PAT CADDELL SAYS: MEDIA HAVE BECOME "ENEMY OF THE AMERICAN PEOPLE"

By Roger Aronoff   September 27, 2012

In remarks to the AIM conference, "ObamaNation: A Day of Truth," on September 21st, former Democratic pollster and analyst Pat Caddell said, "I think we're at the most dangerous time in our political history in terms of the balance of power in the role that the media plays in whether or not we maintain a free democracy." Caddell noted that while First Amendment protections were originally provided to the press so they would protect the liberty and freedom of the public from "organized governmental power," they had clearly relinquished the role of impartial news providers.

Nowhere was this more evident than during the tragic death of a U.S. ambassador in Libya that was covered up for nine days because the press and the administration did not want to admit it was a terrorist attack.

"We've had nine day of lies over what happened because they can't dare say it's a terrorist attack, and the press won't push this," said Caddell. "Yesterday there was not a single piece in The New York Times over the question of Libya. Twenty American embassies, yesterday, are under attack. None of that is on the national news. None of it is being pressed in the papers."

Caddell added that it is one thing for the news to have a biased view, but "It is another thing to specifically decide that you will not tell the American people information they have a right to know."

He closed his talk with these words: "The press's job is to stand in the ramparts and protect the liberty and freedom of all of us from a government and from organized governmental power. When they desert those ramparts and go to serve—to decide that they will now become active participants—when they decide that their job is not simply to tell you who you may vote for, and who you may not, but, worse—and this is the danger of the last two weeks—what truth that you may know, as an American, and what truth you are not allowed to know, they have, then, made themselves a fundamental threat to the democracy, and, in my opinion, made themselves the enemy of the American people. And it is a threat to the very future of this country if…we allow this stuff to go on, and…we've crossed a whole new and frightening slide on the slippery slope this last two weeks, and it needs to be talked about."

You can view a video of Pat Caddell's entire speech by visiting www.aim.org.

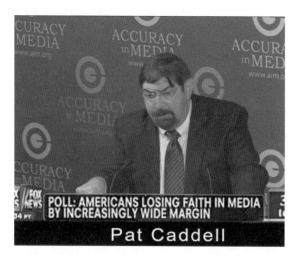

MEDIA BIAS DESIGNED TO SAVE OBAMA'S PRESIDENCY

By Cliff Kincaid   September 18, 2012

The constant refrain from the media that the "anti-Islam" film somehow "triggered" or "sparked" the violence in Libya, Egypt and other countries is a transparent lie that follows on the Obama Administration's attempt to divert attention away from the fact that the "Arab Spring" promoted by Obama has been a complete failure for U.S. interests.

Our media understand that, in the same way that Jimmy Carter lost Iran and America was humiliated during the Iranian hostage crisis, there is a danger that Obama will be perceived to have lost Egypt to the Muslim Brotherhood, as violent demonstrations continue in the Middle East and other Arab/Muslim areas of the world. Hence, attention is being directed to a film that has been on the Internet since July. It is a diversion intended to save Obama's presidency.

Yet, it is significant that Hillary Clinton has been leading the charge against the film, rather than take responsibility for the lack of security in Benghazi, Libya, where the murders of the Americans occurred. Clinton denounced the film and federal authorities directed the apprehension of the filmmaker, using the pretext that he was wanted for questioning about unrelated legal matters.

But this is more than a political ploy by the media to protect Obama. The coordinated attack on the First Amendment threatens the lives of Americans who dare to criticize Islam and who organize to expose Muslim Brotherhood operations on U.S. soil. Coptic Christian Joseph Nassralla, who has been falsely linked in media reports to the content of the film, tells Pamela Geller:

"There has been a campaign of disinformation and smears about the film 'Innocence of Muslims' and my involvement in it. I have been forced to leave my home, and I have received numerous death threats. It grieves me that my intent was to call attention to the relentless, bloody persecution of the Copts, but that issue is of no interest to the media at all."

Despite the media bias, it should be clear to anyone paying even casual attention that Obama has lost Egypt and is now in danger of losing Libya to the Islamists.

And Egypt is lost, despite claims by Wolf Blitzer and others on CNN that Obama has somehow made the Muslim Brotherhood government see the light about the need to protect American interests. There is a "government" in place in Libya, and its officials have directly contradicted the Obama Administration's claims about the "spontaneous" nature of the anti-American violence. This violence, however, demonstrates that the Libyan government either has no power or control over the country, or it is unwilling to confront the Islamists. Under these circumstances, it is only a matter of time before the terrorists are in complete control and eventually take power there officially, just as they have in Egypt.

One thing is certain: the demonstrations will continue, and more Americans will have to go into hiding because of death threats from adherents of the "religion of peace."

Our media could help stop this catastrophe, but they would prefer to save Obama's presidency.

AP PROTECTS OBAMA WHILE ATTACKING CONSERVATIVE FILM

By Cliff Kincaid   August 29, 2012

When Beth Fouhy of the Associated Press (AP) reviewed Dinesh D'Souza's popular film, "2016: Obama's America," she attacked its central claim that Obama's alleged philosophy of anti-colonialism stemmed from the influence of the Kenyan Obama who was mostly absent from the President's life.

Her article, "Fact Check: 'Anti-colonial' Obama not plausible," which ran in hundreds of papers worldwide, conveyed the impression that D'Souza was deliberately misleading the public and distorting the facts about Obama's background.

However, Fouhy ignored the portion of the film featuring an interview with Professor Paul Kengor, a Cold War historian, who discussed Obama's mentor in Hawaii, communist Frank Marshall Davis. The media have always regarded this relationship as taboo. The failure to talk truthfully about Davis constitutes one of the most important and insidious cover-ups in presidential history.

Fouhy clearly preferred that the cover-up continue. Her movie "review," as such, seemed designed to warn people not to take Obama's critics seriously when they questioned his foreign connections.

AIM has argued that Obama's Marxist connection is far more significant than whatever "anti-colonial" views D'Souza suggested he has. Communist parties still engage in subversion and espionage against the United States, sometimes in collaboration with Islamist movements.

Focusing on the movie's faulty claims of Obama's anti-colonialism, Fouhy wrote, "…it's difficult to see how Obama's political leanings could have been so directly shaped by his father, as D'Souza claimed. The elder Obama left his wife and young son, the future president, when Obama was two years old and visited his son only once, when Obama was 10. But D'Souza portrayed that loss as an event that reinforced rather than weakened the president's ties to his father…"

This assertion is reasonable, but Fouhy overlooked D'Souza's inclusion of the interview with Paul Kengor, who had access to Davis's 600-page FBI file and his writings for Communist Party papers. Kengor made the well-documented assertion that it was Davis who most heavily influenced Obama while he was growing up in Hawaii.

While D'Souza's film is flawed in terms of the anti-colonialism angle, Fouhy's strange omission of the Davis matter made her review still more questionable. D'Souza at least seemed to represent, with the Kengor interview, his awareness that there was an alternate view of how Obama turned out.

The Fouhy review was not the first time the major media have refused to address the facts about Obama's ties to the well-known Communist. Several years ago, the AP ran a story about Davis without mentioning the smoking-gun evidence that he was a Communist Party member. The AP then called Davis a "left-leaning black journalist and poet" known for "leftist politics," and someone who might be accused by some of having "allegedly anti-American views."

Fouhy could have set the record straight by citing the Kengor interview or writing about the 600-page FBI file on Davis. Perhaps she realized that the facts were not in dispute and that her best approach was simply to ignore them. This is not real "fact-checking," but the kind of dishonest journalism that helped guarantee a second term for Obama.

PENTAGON CELEBRATES GAY PRIDE DURING TREASON TRIAL

By Cliff Kincaid   July 5, 2012

On June 26, 2012, the Defense Department hosted a Lesbian, Gay, Bisexual and Transgender Pride Month event but failed to include any mention, pro or con, of the most celebrated homosexual soldier in American history, Bradley Manning, who was on trial for treason at that time.

An examination of the transcript shows that no one at the DoD event saw fit to denounce Manning's alleged treachery by leaking classified information to Julian Assange and WikiLeaks. The Washington Post story about the Pentagon "pride" event was also silent about the scandal, as if the Manning case had nothing to do with the conduct of homosexuals in the military.

"i [sic] have sources in the White House re: DADT and the disaster that keeps going on with that… Shin Inouye," Manning wrote in a series of emails that included the name of a top Obama White House official. DADT is a reference to "Don't Ask, Don't Tell," the policy prohibiting open homosexuality in the military.

Manning had been an out-of-the-closet homosexual before its repeal, and had been working with various gay rights and Democratic Party groups. Was he a gay "mole" in the ranks?

Inouye, a former associate of the ACLU office in Washington, D.C., is openly homosexual and handles gay rights issues in the executive office of the president. Before going to the White House, where he serves as Director of Specialty Media, Inouye was a spokesperson for the Presidential Inaugural Committee and, prior to that, was the Constituency Communications Coordinator at the Obama for America campaign.

Gawker, a website that has tackled the topic because of the sex angle, has reported that Manning was close to Inouye. Manning reportedly said of Inouye, "He's a friend of mine," and that a Manning reference to "White House contact (he's tried to sleep with me, uggh)," included a link to a Facebook photo of Inouye in a White House press room. "Strangely," Gawker said about the scandal, "Manning's connection to the D.C. gay establishment, not to mention the White House, has been glossed over."

Our questions include: "Was Manning a pawn of high-level officials in the Obama White House? Who protected him? And why?"

"It's interesting to me that this individual [Manning] was able to get his security clearance even while homosexuality was a court-martial offense," said Chaplain (Col.) Ron Crews, USAR retired, the executive director for the Chaplain Alliance for Religious Liberty.

"As gays serve openly, chaplains report few problems" was the headline over an Associated Press story by David Crary that appeared in papers across the country.

Crews countered that this is the case because chaplains expressing concern about the new policy "have been ordered by their commanders not to speak to the press." He said, "As long as you're in favor of the repeal and the current DoD policy, you can speak to the press."

"I don't think we are getting the full story yet," he added.

That also seems to be the case with the Bradley Manning-Shin Inouye connection. But like so many other Obama scandals, the media are not anxious to get to the bottom of this one.

REPUBLICANS OUTMANEUVERED BY OBAMA AND HOLDER

By Cliff Kincaid   June 11, 2012

Senator John McCain, who lost to President Obama in 2008 in part because he did not want to challenge Obama's personal character or loyalty to the U.S., is now upset over what he calls "…a disturbing stream of articles" that cite "leaked classified or highly-sensitive information…" in an "effort to paint a portrait of President Obama as a strong leader on national security issues…"

The senator went on to say, "The fact that this Administration would aggressively pursue leaks perpetrated by a 22-year old Army private in the 'WikiLeaks' matter and former CIA employees in other leaks cases but apparently sanction leaks made by senior Administration officials for political purposes is simply unacceptable. It also calls for the need for a special counsel to investigate what happened here."

Here, the Senator made two questionable assumptions: 1.)that the administration was determined to aggressively pursue the WikiLeaks matter, and 2.) that "senior Administration officials" were behind the recent leaks, not Obama himself.

In the first place, government prosecutors have ruled out the death penalty in the case of Army intelligence analyst Bradley Manning, the source of the classified WikiLeaks material. This is strange because the leaks constituted the largest release of classified information in history. The trial of Manning, regarded as a hero by the radical left, has been repeatedly delayed and now won't occur until November 2012. Then, after the election, it wouldn't be surprising to see the government dropping some of the charges against him.

Secondly, Attorney General Eric Holder did not bring charges against Wikileaks founder Julian Assange, who allegedly received the stolen documents from Manning and was therefore part of a conspiracy to commit espionage. Like Manning, Assange is a hero to much of Obama's political "progressive" base.

McCain's decision to accuse administration officials, rather than Obama himself, of the leaks to The New York Times, was an assumption that enabled the senator to avoid questioning Obama's personal patriotism. McCain fought for his country in wartime but politically he wants to "play nice."

McCain requested a special counsel independent of the Justice Department to investigate the leaks. Holder outflanked McCain, appointing U.S. Attorney for the District of Columbia Ronald C. Machen Jr. and U.S. Attorney for the District of Maryland Rod J. Rosenstein to conduct the inquiry and "follow all appropriate investigative leads within the Executive and Legislative branches of government." Since not even McCain suggested the President personally did the leaking, it wasn't appropriate to investigate Obama himself. As a result, Obama was, once again, off the hook. Congress will hold hearings, but they will go nowhere because the administration will claim an investigation is already underway.

Nobody doubts that McCain, who was tortured by the communists when he was a POW during the Vietnam War, believes in his country. But his decision to give Obama the benefit of the doubt makes no sense.

MEDIA OBSESS ABOUT TRUMP AND FIND NOTHING CONTROVERSIAL ON THE LEFT

By Roger Aronoff   May 30, 2012

On a day when Barack Obama bestowed the Presidential Medal of Freedom on a socialist, Dolores Huerta, and just days after left-wing activist Al Sharpton compared Republicans to Hitler, the media were consumed with the horror of projected Republican nominee Mitt Romney sharing a stage with Donald Trump, who had the temerity to ask questions about President Obama's birth certificate and place of birth. The usual double standard was on open display.

Nearly every hour of programming on MSNBC and CNN featured the same message: How could Mitt Romney agree to hold a fundraiser with Donald Trump, who has continued making comments about Obama's birth certificate?

Yet how many times have these same networks, particularly MSNBC, overlooked Obama's past and current associations with everyone from unrepentant terrorist Bill Ayers, to "comedian" Bill Maher, to the preacher of hate, Jeremiah Wright, to self-described communist Van Jones?

Roger Kimball, the Editor and Publisher of The New Criterion and head of Encounter Books, wrote an excellent piece for Pajamas Media titled, "Who Is Barack Obama? The Question that Won't Go Away," in which he questioned Obama's radical ties from the past, his sealed records on everything from college transcripts to why he gave up his law license, to another controversy that the mainstream media wouldn't touch: the biographical pamphlet circulated by his literary agent, which said that he was born in Kenya. It remained that way for 17 years, undergoing several revisions, including after Obama became a U.S. senator, but it never changed his place of birth as Kenya until just before he decided to run for president. The explanations have been that it was a fact-checking error, or a typo, neither of which made any sense. Are we to believe that they pulled that fact out of thin air, that someone was confused when writing it, that Obama never saw it and asked to correct it?

And what about the latest Jeremiah Wright scandal? Edward Klein, former editor of The New York Times Magazine, revealed in his book, *The Amateur*, that Wright was offered $150,000 to remain quiet during the Obama presidential campaign in 2008. More specifically, he was offered the money in an email "if he would shut-up and not criticize Obama anymore," Klein told Sean Hannity on his radio show.

Klein named the person who made the offer as Dr. Eric Whitaker, the vice president of the University of Chicago Medical Center and a "member of Obama's very tight inner circle." Klein pointed out that "Whitaker's hospital is the same one that paid First Lady Michelle Obama $316,962 a year to handle community affairs for the University of Chicago Medical Center while her husband served in the U.S. Senate."

The issue here is a complete double standard, wherein Obama is given a pass on almost any of his associations, especially those on the far Left. And when legitimate questions are raised, they are dismissed under the umbrella of birtherism.

WASHINGTON POST HIRES LEFT-WING BLOGGER TO BASH CONSERVATIVES

By Cliff Kincaid   May 21, 2012

The decline of The Washington Post was again on display when a Post blogger reported that a literary agency representing Obama had committed a mere "typo" when it identified him as being born in Kenya.

Conservative blogger Doug Ross notes that this "typo" ran for 17 years, and that the Kenyan birthplace changed just weeks after Obama announced his presidential run. Ross used the Wayback Archive to explore the exact transformations of Obama's biography on his agent's website.

A "typo" would be when someone mistakenly types Osama instead of Obama. These things are usually quickly picked up by proofreaders or editors. The claim in the pamphlet that Obama was "born in Kenya" rather than Hawaii or any other place cannot be considered a typo, especially because it has to be assumed that Obama and/or his agent approved and wrote the copy.

But here's how Post blogger Rachel Weiner reported the controversy: "…the Drudge Report prominently featured a blog post about a 1991 literary agency pamphlet advertising Obama as 'born in Kenya.' On Friday afternoon, the story is still close to the top of the page, though a former staffer at the agency has explained that it was her typo."

A "typo" that ran for 17 years?

The question then is: was the information about Kenya true? Was it made up by someone trying to portray Obama as Kenyan-born? Was this part of an affirmative action ploy on his behalf?

The "blog post" was from Breitbart.com, which went out of its way to declare that it believed Obama was born in Hawaii, not Kenya. Nevertheless, Weiner called it "birtherism," which is a derogatory term that is supposed to suggest that questions about Obama's birthplace are crazy.

We are dealing here with a President, now a candidate for re-election, who claims to be a Christian but yet his own minister, Jeremiah Wright, says he is not sure that Obama converted from Islam to Christianity. Obama said he was mentored in Hawaii by a mysterious person named "Frank," who turned out to be a member of the Communist Party.

Faced with the truth about "Frank," the Obama campaign said he was a black civil rights activist. This is like saying a "typo" was not corrected for 17 years.

The claim that Obama was "born in Kenya" cannot be dismissed out of hand, even though there is a controversial "birth certificate" from Obama declaring he was born in Hawaii. Nothing the candidate says should be taken at face value, but the Post believes in Obama, no matter where he was born, and is determined to dismiss any questions that cast doubt on his life story, as he presents or changes it. That is Rachel Weiner's mission, now that the campaign is underway.

A legitimate reporter should know that a "typo" is not something that runs for 17 years and misrepresents something as important as a place where someone was born.

THE NEW YORK TIMES' WAR ON POLICE

By Cliff Kincaid   April 27, 2012

At The New York Times annual meeting on April 25, Chairman and Chief Executive Officer Arthur Sulzberger Jr. denied that his paper was waging a war on the New York City Police Department and its commissioner, Ray Kelly. The denials are not convincing.

As I arrived in New York City for the annual meeting, the reason for the recent intensity of this campaign became apparent. Other papers were full of stories about how Kelly, who is very popular with city residents, is being pushed by New York City Republican officials to run for mayor.

The New York Daily News is reporting that Kelly's job approval rating is at 77%, while his 63% favorability rating among city voters was "by far the highest of anyone considering a mayoral run next year."

The Times is determined to do something about that.

On the same day as the annual meeting, the Times published a puff piece on how New York City Council Speaker Christine Quinn, the leading Democrat for the office, could become the city's first homosexual mayor.

This is somehow supposed to be a qualification for higher office.

In a story headlined, "After 11 Years, a Police Leader Hits Turbulence," the Times on February 3 played down Kelly's success in fighting crime and terrorism, and savaged him with everything but the proverbial kitchen sink. The Times assigned not one, not two, but three reporters—N. R. Kleinfield, Al Baker and Joseph Goldstein—to the story. The charges included:

- Kelly is "confronted with a steady drip of

troublesome episodes," including officers "fixing traffic tickets, running guns and disparaging civilians on Facebook," and accusations that the Police Department "encourages officers to question minorities on the streets indiscriminately."

- Kelly these days "seems to exude remoteness."

- Kelly "is rarely expansive or publicly introspective."

- "With his stubbled crew cut and muscled look, he is the picture of the prototypical police officer. Beneath his piercing eyes, a grimace appears to have been ironed onto his face."

Kelly was even faulted for not taking vacations: "Except for a few long weekends, he has not had a vacation in years. He goes to bed knowing his security detail is under orders to wake him if an officer fires his weapon or is shot."

This concern about public safety and his officers was portrayed as unbecoming.

The real agenda became clear later in the story. It said that government agencies, academics and reporters "complain that the department is unwilling to provide insight into its workings—even statistics on lower-level crime or Mr. Kelly's daily schedule."

So Kelly doesn't spill his guts to the Times and tell them about his schedule on any given day. Perhaps he is suspicious of the press and their agenda. He should be.

As I mentioned to Sulzberger, after failing to get any kind of apology for his war-on-cops campaign, public support for Kelly demonstrates that the efforts of the paper to undermine Kelly and the police department have not been too terribly effective.

It is becoming increasingly clear that the person who needs to go is Sulzberger, not Kelly.

INTERVIEW WITH DENEEN BORELLI—
AUTHOR OF BLACKLASH

By Roger Aronoff   April 13, 2012

In an interview with Accuracy in Media, author, political activist and Fox News contributor Deneen Borelli called Al Sharpton an "ambulance chaser," citing the Tawana Brawley case. She also dove into the Tea Party movement, affirmative action, the Democrats' hold over the black vote, school choice and ObamaCare. Borelli is the author of the new book *Blacklash: How Obama and the Left are Driving Americans to the Government Plantation*.

Borelli referred to the Trayvon Martin case as "a very tragic situation."

"My heart truly goes out to this young man's parents," she said. "But, sadly, we have some individuals who are really trying to gain from this tragedy...The other thing I want to point out is that the tone of this incident has been set at the top, from President Obama, when he made his comment, saying that his child would look like him...I do believe there is a pattern in Obama's comments where he has chosen racial tension in our country instead of calming racial tension, and I find that very concerning."

Below, in italics, are excerpts from the half-hour interview, which was conducted on March 29, 2012, well before the special prosecutor charged George Zimmerman with second-degree murder in this case.

"*...There is a monopoly on the message. The monopoly is generally from the black establishment—I'm talking about Jesse Jackson, Al Sharpton, different black publications...This message of victimization, and times that blacks need special treatment when, in fact, that's all a lie...Don't just follow the crowd! Learn on your own, and then make an informed decision.*

Too many Americans…are afraid to be true to what they're really thinking about President Obama and his failed policies. When you think about when the Tea Party movement came on the scene in 2009, how the liberal Left tried its hardest to demonize and discredit the movement, calling anyone involved with the movement "racist," "rednecks," and "extremists"—I've been involved with the Tea Party movement since Day One…these individuals are concerned about the direction our country is going in, they're concerned about the massive growth of government.

I think the Democrat Party gets way too much credit for the passage of the Civil Rights Act, and, when you think about the last election, 2008, with Obama, a lot of blacks did vote for him simply because of his skin color. But I say Martin Luther King— "content of character," not skin color.

There are a number of black conservatives who are what I call "closet conservatives," and it's because they are afraid of being targeted and criticized by their friends, their co-workers.

Getting back to Al Sharpton, I call him an "ambulance chaser," I write about how he ruined many lives…There's a lack of accountability here. I hope people will understand what their endgame is—this is just really for their agenda, to monopolize on situations such as the one that's going on in Florida."

MSNBC TO HAVE MATTHEWS & CO. HOST THIS YEAR'S ELECTION COVERAGE

By Roger Aronoff   March 20, 2012

Unlike in 2008, MSNBC is planning to have Chris Matthews, along with the rest of the primetime lineup of MSNBC, host the 2012 presidential election coverage. This includes the presidential debates in September and October, and election night itself.

When it came up in 2008, MSNBC decided to pull their two top hosts, Matthews and Keith Olbermann, from anchoring the presidential debates and election night. But this year is different. The primetime lineup is going to be doing anchoring and analysis: one stop shopping. Despite repeated requests for further explanation, so far we have gotten no answer.

The big question is, can Matthews resist revealing the "thrill going up my leg" when President Obama speaks. How about Al Sharpton, Ed Schultz, Lawrence O'Donnell, and Rachel Maddow? Is there no concern at the network that every one of their hosts are strongly partisan Obama supporters, and extremely hostile to all things conservative and Republican? Watch any of their shows on any night if you have any doubts. (Keith Olbermann has moved on to Al Gore's Learning-Impaired Channel, also known as Current-TV.)

In early September of 2008, shortly after the two parties had completed their conventions, MSNBC stated on its website that it would "replace the team of Chris Matthews and Keith Olbermann as anchors of its live political coverage for the rest of the presidential campaign season. David Gregory, NBC News' chief White House correspondent, will be the primary host of coverage of the presidential and vice presidential debates coming up over the next two months, as well as election night, said Phil Griffin, MSNBC's president."

The New York Times' Brian Stelter reported on the story and found that there was a lot more to it: "The change," wrote Stelter, "which comes in the home stretch of the long election cycle—is a direct result of tensions associated with the channel's perceived shift to the political left."

But the question remains, will that lineup of partisan pundits dispassionately analyze comments critical of President Obama and his policies, and resist jumping to his defense? Not likely. Someone in management should step up and make the journalistically sound move, like they did in 2008, of putting less partisan newsmen, like David Gregory or Brian Williams, in the anchor chairs for this year's election coverage.

To the extent that GE has any say, this remains a possibility. The New York Post is reporting that GE's CEO Jeffrey Immelt, a life-long Republican who has been serving as the head of President Obama's Jobs Council and as an economic adviser, has told friends that he is privately pulling for Mitt Romney to get the Republican nomination and to defeat President Obama.

According to the article by Charles Gasparino, Immelt won't admit it publicly, but privately he is "dismayed that, even after three years on the job, President Obama hasn't moved to the center, but instead further left." He says that Immelt is "appalled by everything from the president's class-warfare to his continued belief that big government is the key to economic salvation."

MEDIA MATTERS, OR DOES IT?

By Roger Aronoff   March 6, 2012

The news for Media Matters keeps getting worse and worse. After weeks of stonewalling about the excellent Daily Caller series that broke on February 12, 2012, Media Matters founder David Brock and his co-author, Ari Rabin-Havt, of the new book, *The Fox Effect*, have selectively responded to some of the allegations made in the series.

According to one of the sources who talked to The Daily Caller, "Every Tuesday evening, meanwhile, a representative from Media Matters attends the Common Purpose Project meeting at the Capitol Hilton…where dozens of progressive organizations formulate strategy, often with a representative from the Obama White House."

While their tax exempt status with the IRS has been challenged in the past, it is coming under renewed scrutiny.

Brock heads up the Super PAC, American Bridge 21st Century, as well as Media Matters, and the two are housed in the same Washington D.C. offices.

According to Fox News documents, Brock was being threatened by a former domestic partner with information on Media Matters' donors and the IRS. This might provide useful information if Congress actually investigates.

In a potential financial controversy, Media Matters has collected $365,000 in ill-gotten gains from three foundations that convicted Ponzi-scheme operator Bernie Madoff had "invested" in.

As reported by Alana Goodman, now writing for Commentary: "Harvard Law Professor Alan Dershowitz, who was a key supporter of Obama in 2008, told WOR710 today that he could not vote for President Obama's reelection unless the president cuts ties with the controversial anti-Israel group Media Matters."

She then quoted Dershowitz as saying, "Let's have a full and open debate on this, but to the extent that the Obama administration associates with these bigots [at Media Matters], they're going to lose a lot of support among Christians, Jews and others who think that American support for Israel is in the best interest of the United States…"

Media Matters normally has a lot to say in response to their critics, but their silence speaks volumes about these latest accusations from The Daily Caller, Fox News, and Alan Dershowitz.

On February 27th, there was an authors night at Politics and Prose. It was Brock's first public appearance since The Daily Caller series broke, and since Dershowitz had made his comments. The first question of the evening was whether or not they stand by the rhetoric of senior staffer MJ Rosenberg.

Rabin-Havt gave an indirect, rambling answer, saying that he is personally a Zionist and "Israel is an issue that has a deep and heartfelt meaning to me."

When asked to respond to the Daily Caller series in general, Rabin-Havt said, "I'm not going to respond to an article that's basically filled up with just crap."

While Media Matters was holding regular meetings and phone calls with White House staff, they were also coordinating with various journalists, including at MSNBC and The Washington Post.

The relationship between Media Matters and the White House makes it very unlikely that any sort of meaningful investigation from the executive branch, including the IRS, will occur. Unfortunately, the mainstream media have shown no interest in even acknowledging that this scandal exists, much less applying pressure for Congressional hearings.

MEDIA PARTNERS IN CRIME WITH WIKILEAKS?

By Cliff Kincaid   February 28, 2012

Gary Pruitt, President, Chief Executive Officer and Chairman of the Board of The McClatchy Company, insists the U.S. newspaper publisher "must maintain the highest standards of ethical conduct." But how does this comport with being a "partner" of WikiLeaks, the controversial website that has just published stolen emails from the private company known as Stratfor?

WikiLeaks has listed McClatchy as one of its "public partners in the investigation" of Stratfor. Another American "partner" is Rolling Stone, the rock & roll magazine.

The hacker group Anonymous, which is under FBI investigation, has taken credit for the data theft. WikiLeaks founder Julian Assange is himself a computer hacker and maintains close ties to the Russian government.

George Friedman, founder and CEO of Stratfor, which obtains information about and analyzes world events for private companies and U.S. Government agencies, says the theft and publication of the emails are "deplorable, unfortunate, and illegal" actions.

James Asher, Washington, D.C. bureau chief for McClatchy Newspapers, says his company wasn't involved in the theft and hasn't decided what is newsworthy about the documents they have received.

Asher is in charge of 40 reporters and editors in Washington and around the globe.

Stratfor CEO Friedman has cautioned the media about using the material, saying, "Some of the emails may be forged or altered to include inaccuracies. Some may be authentic. We will not validate either, nor will we explain the thinking that went into them."

It is not surprising that Stratfor would cover the case, since Assange is reportedly under investigation by the U.S. Government and one of his alleged sources, Army Private First Class Bradley Manning, is on trial for stealing classified information and aiding the enemy.

Some of the documents concern counter-terrorism operations in the Middle East and the vulnerability of top-secret facilities to terrorist attack.

One of the alleged emails from Stratfor refers to a secret U.S. Government indictment of Assange. But there is no independent evidence that such an indictment has been handed down.

Asked if he would mind somebody stealing his emails and releasing them to the public, Asher said his emails weren't that interesting. When I asked to see them, he laughed and said, "It sounds to me like you have an agenda, sir."

Asked if he thought WikiLeaks had an agenda, he said, "I don't care if WikiLeaks has an agenda. I don't evaluate information based on the agenda of the people who give it to us. I evaluate the information based on how accurate and real it is, and whether it has news value."

Asked if McClatchy had done a story on WikiLeaks founder Julian Assange working for Moscow-funded Russia Today (RT) television, a controversial arrangement that raises questions about his political orientation, Asher said he wasn't aware of that information.

However, some independent commentators have started raising questions about Assange's agenda and loyalties.

The implication is that Assange is a Russian agent whose anti-American mission is now out in the open for all to see—except that his U.S. media "partners" may not want to investigate this part of the story.

FREE SPEECH FOR CONSERVATIVES

By Cliff Kincaid   February 20, 2012

Patrick J. Buchanan, who has been a major figure in the conservative movement for over 40 years, was fired from MSNBC after the Conservative Political Action Conference (CPAC) concluded in Washington, D.C.

Buchanan was not a featured speaker at CPAC, but his former colleague, Joe Scarborough, was. Scarborough, the co-host of a little-watched MSNBC program called "Morning Joe," is a former Republican congressman who pleases the liberals by making sure he doesn't sound too conservative on the air.

Although Scarborough's real mission was to introduce Rep. Paul Ryan (R-WI) at a banquet, he ended up taking shots at then-GOP presidential candidate Newt Gingrich (who was not in attendance). For his part, Scarborough posted photos of himself at CPAC, under the title, "Morning Joe Invades CPAC."

While Buchanan's magazine, The American Conservative, was at CPAC, Buchanan was not, in part due to his criticism of America's foreign wars and pro-Israel foreign policy in the George W. Bush years. Unfortunately for Buchanan, he was forced off the air essentially by the same left-wing forces that previously forced out Glenn Beck, who departed from Fox News because of his scrutiny of anti-American hedge fund billionaire George Soros. Although Buchanan appeared on Sean Hannity's show to defend himself, the trouble for Hannity was that Buchanan followed Glenn Beck out the door from their employer at Fox News (which also employs Hannity).

While Buchanan was in the Reagan White House as communications director, I filled in as the conservative co-host of a then-popular CNN program, "Crossfire." Buchanan was the conservative co-host and Tom Braden was the liberal co-host. The "crossfire" aspect meant that there were conservative and liberal guests who sat in the middle, getting questions from both sides.

The show was cancelled and a true "crossfire" on the issues is not permitted anymore by some important media organizations that fear the Left. Only this year was the show revived with hosts Newt Gingrich, S.E. Cupp, Stephanie Cutter and Van Jones, in a poor attempt to salvage CNN's ratings.

On his Politico blog, Scarborough issued a joint statement with Mika Brzezinski lamenting Buchanan's firing. The statement mentioned how "Mika and I strongly disagree with this outcome" and closed with, "We understand that the parting was amicable. Still, we will miss Pat."

It is also significant that Al Sharpton, who made false racial allegations against white police officers in the notorious Tawana Brawley case, continues his gig on MSNBC while Buchanan was fired. After all, unlike Sharpton, Buchanan has the intellectual ammunition to win his arguments.

It was also disappointing to see Andrew Breitbart's Big-Journalism.com linking to an article that called Buchanan an anti-Semite. The link was to a Pajamas Media piece claiming that Buchanan was fired for the wrong reason, which implied that he should have been fired for a different reason.

As for Joe Scarborough, CPAC should repel his "invasion" the next time he tries to breach the gates. Today, he is a "token conservative" and nothing else.

CBS PROUDLY ACCEPTS AIM'S AWARD, DESPITE CONTROVERSY

By Roger Aronoff   February 11, 2012

Accuracy in Media presented its annual Reed Irvine Awards for Investigative and Grassroots Journalism amidst a trumped-up controversy reported in The Washington Post, Politico and Big Journalism. The awards were presented to Sharyl Attkisson of CBS News for her investigative reporting on Operation Fast and Furious, as well as Solyndra and other "green energy" projects; and Dana Loesch, Editor-in-chief of Andrew Breitbart's Big Journalism.com, for her tireless work as a grassroots journalist.

The pro-Democratic Party media watchdog, Media Matters, tried to pressure Attkisson and CBS to back out of the awards. They claimed her reporting was shoddy and that CBS shouldn't allow her to accept an award from a partisan group such as AIM. Yet as AIM's Cliff Kincaid recently exposed, the head of Media Matters, David Brock, has created a so-called Democratic "Super PAC" aimed at defeating Republicans.

A few hours before the event, Ms. Attkisson contacted AIM to say she was called away on assignment, and Chris Isham (the Washington bureau chief for CBS News) was sent to accept the award on her behalf. Chris was very gracious in accepting the award, saying, "Sharyl was very sorry not to be here today. She is traveling out of town on assignment. I am going to accept this award on her behalf and on behalf of CBS News. Sharyl will be donating the proceeds of this award ($1,000) to the family of Border Patrol Agent Brian Terry." He explained that it was Terry's death in December of 2010 that inspired whistleblowers to discuss Fast and Furious with Atkisson and members of

Congress, which generated the story that really allowed us and congressional investigators to drill down on this operation. He said that "CBS News is very proud of Sharyl's groundbreaking reporting, as you've described it," saying it "represents the best at CBS News."

Newsbusters' Tim Graham gave a great analysis of how the "double standard" media have no problem accepting awards from liberal groups that overwhelmingly favor liberal journalists. He gave the example of Rachel Maddow receiving Planned Parenthood's "Maggie Award." He added, "Some journalism professors would try to suggest that journalists should only accept awards like the Peabody Awards or the Pulitzer Prizes—even when those judgment panels are dominated by liberal media and political elites."

Media Matters acted as if they thought their campaign had succeeded, writing an article entitled "CBS Pulls Attkisson From CPAC Award Event." But as Big Journalism's Dan Riehl pointed out, they offered no evidence to support their claim that this was anything other than what Attkisson and Isham had said. The Huffington Post and Politico also wrote about the event and focused on the fact that Attkisson didn't attend the ceremony. "If Media Matters wanted to report that CBS was somehow behind Attkisson not attending in person to receive the award," wrote Riehl, "it's their responsibility to provide documentation of same, assuming truth matters at MMfA. As many believe, their handling of the non-event indicates truth doesn't matter to Eric Boehlert and Media Matters at all."

MSNBC'S USUAL SUSPECTS AND PLANS FOR THE DEMOCRATS TO GO "NASTY"

By Roger Aronoff   February 2, 2012

The NBC brand, which used to have much higher standards, has been damaged by its cable news division MSNBC. One such example was MSNBC's analysis of the Florida primary, which demanded retractions and corrections that never came.

On January 31st, the day of the Florida primary, Chris Matthews was on with New York magazine's John Heilemann and Huffington Post's Howard Fineman.

Heilemann said the 2008 campaign between Hillary Clinton and Barack Obama was never as vicious as the 2012 GOP nomination. Heilemann, along with Mark Halperin, wrote the liberals' favorite book on the election, *Game Change*.

Heilemann said, "There was not a negative ad run between Clinton-Obama until March in that race. We've seen negative ads [in this Florida primary] on an unprecedented scale."

But Heilemann was wrong because a Google search turned up loads of examples of negative attacks between the two, and well before March of 2008. Here is a small sampling of stories about negative ads, during Heilemann's time frame:

From CBS, on February 16, 2008: "<u>Obama Counters Clinton's Negative Ad</u>;"

From ABC on December 31, 2007: "<u>Obama Launches First Negative Ad</u>;"

From The Young Turks on the Hillary Clinton: the "<u>3 a.m. wake-up call</u>" ad;

A YouTube from a debate in which <u>Hillary accused Obama of plagiarism</u>; and

From CNN: "<u>Clinton camp pulls negative ad in South Carolina</u>."

The key difference was that when Hillary and Obama called each other liars, or plagiarists, or not ready, or unfit for the office, the media usually tried to keep it from becoming a media circus. The liberal media, especially MSNBC, wanted the Republican nomination to be as ugly as possible.

Howard Fineman later said that he had spoken to some Democrats close to the White House. He said, "They've been assuming Romney is the candidate... *So if you think it was nasty now, wait till you see what the Democrats have planned for Mitt Romney*".

Then Matthews accused Romney of committing the crime of hiding his assets in the Cayman Islands. He accused Romney of "shipping his money overseas to hide it from the IRS."

Matthews works for MSNBC, part of the NBC family, <u>which in 2010 made $14.2 billion</u> worldwide, and $5.1 billion on its U.S. operations, according to The New York Times. It paid zero federal income taxes in the U.S., but claimed a $3.2 billion benefit through lobbying, write-offs and loopholes. GE had owned 80% of NBC Universal, but today owns 49% of NBC. And GE CEO Jeffrey Immelt heads President Obama's Council on Jobs and Competitiveness.

This made Matthews a hypocrite because he accused Romney of hiding money from the IRS, while working for a company that avoids paying U.S. taxes. Furthermore, <u>a majority of GE's more than 300,000 employees are based overseas</u>, after shuttering 28 manufacturing plants in the

U.S. between 2005 and 2009. Yet GE's CEO is, ironically, the head of the President's Jobs Council?

According to <u>a column</u> by the widely respected economist Alan Reynolds, Romney's assets are legal, they have nothing to hide, and they have "no choice about how or where the money is invested."

And that was the point that Matthews foolishly missed.

NEW YORK TIMES PROMOTES FREEDOM FOR TERRORIST

By Cliff Kincaid   January 16, 2012

Sara Bennett, an attorney for convicted communist terrorist Judith Clark, was optimistic that her client benefitted from a New York Times Magazine article that advocated her release from prison. "Did I think they did a good job for my client? Yes I do," she said in a telephone interview.

A member of the Weather Underground, Clark was involved in a terrorist assault that killed Nyack, New York Police Sgt. Edward O'Grady, Patrolman Waverly Brown and Brinks guard Peter Paige. A website, memorial and scholarship have been created in their honor.

Tom Robbins, a former Village Voice writer now at the CUNY Graduate School of Journalism who visited Clark in prison, wrote the Times story, "Judith Clark's Radical Transformation." Clark, he wrote, "is a model for what's possible in prison" and has shown "genuine remorse."

The story also emphasizes her attendance at Jewish services in prison.

Incredibly, the Times story confirms that Clark earned educational degrees behind bars, courtesy of "tuition aid" provided by the taxpayers. These degrees are also said to be proof of her turnaround in prison.

Tina Trent, an advocate for crime victims, said Clark's "fake degrees" were a sad attempt to be released from prison. Agreeing with Trent was former FBI informant Larry Grathwohl, who infiltrated the Weather Underground and knew Clark.

"Here's another 60s and 70s terrorist who has found God and has changed her life," he said sarcastically. "The New

York Times article contained very little in the way of repentance and only lightly touched on the families and children of the officers killed that day."

The murderous assault took place during a Brinks truck robbery of $1.6 million on October 20, 1981. Clark was sentenced to three consecutive terms of 25 years to life, totaling 75 years in prison, for three murder convictions. She is currently in state custody at the Bedford Hills , NY Correctional Facility.

Clark tried every possible legal maneuver to get out of jail, such as blaming inadequate legal representation when she represented herself during her trial, in addition to asking for "dramatic readings" of clemency letters by Hollywood supporters like Kevin Kline and Steve Buscemi. None of these efforts resulted in clemency.

David Horowitz, the former communist-turned-conservative thinker, writer and activist, argued that if Clark were a "truly remorseful terrorist" she would have exposed her former comrades "and who their networks are, and what they actually did—not just what they got caught doing." Telling the truth, said Horowitz, would act as "an authentic form of atonement" for her deeds.

But Clark's attorney Sara Bennett had a left-wing background of her own. She used to work for the Liberation News Service (LNS), which was allied with the forerunner to the Weather Underground, the Students for a Democratic Society (SDS).

A photographer for LNS, David Fenton, is currently a high-powered public relations representative for the radical left, including such organizations as the AFL-CIO and

MoveOn.org and figures like billionaire George Soros.

THE MEDIA OBSESSION WITH AND ABUSE OF POLLS

By Roger Aronoff   December 14, 2011

We should be very skeptical of most polls, and observant of how the media try to use them to shape our opinions, rather than reflect them. In addition, the liberal media are eager to have a role in picking the candidate who they look most forward to pummeling in a general election against President Obama.

One thing most of these polls have in common is that they interview more Democrats than Republicans, and claim to adjust the outcome by "weighting" to account for the difference. However, out of 100 people surveyed in an NBC/WSJ poll, showing Romney and Gingrich in a statistical tie with Obama (within the margin of error), 42 voted for Obama last time, while only 32 voted for McCain. So right there, the results become skewed. The weighting process generally doesn't provide a sufficient adjustment, although the pollsters would argue otherwise, especially when you consider that the largest number of those polled identify themselves as Independents.

It appears that poll results have something to offer everyone. Statistics can be massaged to make the point that the analyst wants. However, presidential primary polls that are more popularity contests within political parties are not good predictors of what the voters are going to do. In poll results that measure ideological commitment by asking the same questions month after month and year after year, trust is built up or eroded over longer periods of time. But even then there are often contradictions.

For example, a recent CBS poll showed that 75% of those surveyed said the country is on the wrong track while only 21% say it's on the right track. However, 57% believe the President is a strong leader. And once again, the numbers are stacked to favor the Democrats, since 32% of those polled were Democrats while only 27% were Republicans.

Obama's job approval rating was 44%, with 46% disapproval, which as Bob Schieffer pointed out on the CBS Evening News when they released this poll on December 9, 2011, "you have to go all the way back to Jimmy Carter to find a president whose approval rating was this low at this point in his presidency."

Obama regularly takes solace in the fact that his ratings are much higher than those of Congress, which he and his spokesmen, both in the White House and in the media, suggest is because it is a Republican-controlled Congress. Republicans do control the House, but not the Senate.

The current polls may well prove to be a dead-on predictor of this year's Republican nominating process, and Newt Gingrich might wrap it up by March. But if recent history is a guide, expect the unexpected in the coming months. New rules put in place by the Republicans promise to make this race different from past races. Time to buckle up and see where this ride takes us.

MEDIA WHITEWASH BARNEY FRANK'S SCANDALOUS LEGACY

By Cliff Kincaid   December 5, 2011

The publication that published scores of stories about sexual charges against Republican Herman Cain whitewashed the documented sex scandal that almost brought down Democratic Representative Barney Frank (MA), saying that a prostitute Frank hired through a "hot bottom" ad was just his "friend." Rep. Frank has announced he will not run for another term.

The Politico story about Frank depicts the congressman as one of Congress's "most able legislators." The author, Jonathan Allen, is a former staffer to a Democratic member of Congress.

Frank's "friend," also described as a "former lover," was a prostitute who Frank had taken into the House gymnasium, in violation of House rules. The prostitute, Stephen Gobie, said they had sex in the gym.

While Frank's role in the financial crisis has been noted by some publications and commentators, the sex scandal that could have forced his resignation or expulsion from Congress was mostly ignored. Frank was reprimanded by the House for using his congressional office to do favors for Gobie, but he refused to resign his seat in Congress.

Evidence showed that Frank found Gobie through a "hot bottom" ad in the Washington Blade, a homosexual paper. The ad for Gobie's sexual services said, "Exceptionally good-looking, personable, muscular athlete is available. Hot bottom plus large endowment equals a good time."

Allen, who covers Congress, previously co-authored a story accusing some Republicans of being "obsessed" with banning homosexual marriage. He was formerly a top staffer at Democratic Representative Debbie Wasserman

Schultz's political action committee. His wife is Communications Director for Democratic Senator Kay Hagan.

The story ran in the print edition under the front-page headline, "Frank Legacy: 'One of a Kind.'" The online version carried the headline, "Barney Frank's parting shot: Congress is broken."

Although Politico tried to suggest Frank knew nothing of what Gobie was doing in Frank's own apartment, Gobie testified that Frank knew everything. The House Ethics Committee investigation of this scandal took Frank's word for it. It also accepted Frank's claim that no sex with Gobie occurred in the House gym, even though Gobie had provided an accurate description of the layout of the gym.

Their "friendship" was initially a matter of exchanging money for sex. Later, Gobie did personal errands for Frank for cash, amounting to several thousand dollars.

Making the Politico treatment look almost objective by comparison, Robert G. Kaiser of The Washington Post wrote an article praising Frank and saying that "We have maintained friendly relations ever since, so readers should be on notice that this article may want for objectivity."

Kaiser wrote that Frank was "an accomplished legislator, a congressman who made a difference. He was usually the smartest man in the room, and the funniest."

As far as Politico is concerned, Frank has emerged unscathed as a statesman, even after all of the documented scandals. Republicans, on the other hand, are going to be endlessly pilloried with charges that may or may not be true.

The treatment of Frank is another reason why Politico's credibility is taking a nose dive.

CHRIS MATTHEWS: GAFFE MACHINE

By Roger Aronoff   November 28, 2011

When Chris Matthews was on The Tonight Show in November, 2011 plugging his new book about John F. Kennedy, he started off with a good laugh at Governor Rick Perry's expense. Governor Perry had, just the night before, experienced his 53-second brain-freeze during the GOP presidential debate when he forgot the third item on a list of three government agencies that he said he would work to eliminate if he became president.

Later in the conversation, Jay Leno asked Matthews if that was "the worst faux pas" he had seen "in modern debate history." Matthews responded that it was "a hell of a list." He then cited Dan Quayle for his spelling of the word potato.

Any others? Matthews came up with the Quayle anecdote that topped his list.

"The best one, I guess, was Dan Quayle, comparing himself to Jack Kennedy. And Lloyd Bentsen said, 'you're no Jack Kennedy.' That was a home run for that guy. He was never heard of again, by the way..."

All Quayle had said was that he had just as much experience in Congress as Jack Kennedy had when he won the presidency in 1960. But Quayle's comment was what prompted vice presidential candidate Lloyd Bentsen, who was running with Michael Dukakis in 1988, to come back with his famous line.

But Matthews still wasn't through with his gaffes and brain freezes. Jay asked about the other (than Rick Perry) candidates. This was the day after Herman Cain had come out and said he had never acted inappropriately with anyone, when asked if he had ever sexually harassed anyone.

"Well *Perry's* got, don't you wish you had his self confidence. This guy comes out and says 'I have never done anything wrong.'"

At this point it wasn't clear if Matthews meant to say Perry or Cain. But he quickly cleared that up when he added, "I don't know if he's telling the truth about how he behaved with these women."

During an interview with Alex Witt on MSNBC to plug his Kennedy book, Matthews expressed his frustration with Obama's presidency, before falling back in line. It was perhaps his harshest criticism to date: "There's nothing to root for. What are we trying to do in this administration? ... What's he going to do in his second term, more of this? Is this it? Is this as good as it gets? Where are we going?"

He added that "[Obama] has not said one thing about what he'd do in his second term...." Just tell us," he said.

Matthews then reverted to his "thrill up my leg" persona: "Just tell us, Commander," he implored Obama, "Give us our orders and tell us where we're going. Give us the mission. And he hasn't done it."

The moral of this story is that if you're going to appear on TV, without your teleprompter, to make fun of other people for their gaffes, faux pas, and brain freezes, try not to have too many of your own.

MEDIA PORTRAY OBAMA AS REAGANESQUE

By Cliff Kincaid   November 17, 2011

President Obama is being portrayed as a "peace through strength" Ronald Reagan Republican as he travels abroad. This propaganda has the effect of playing down China's military build-up and aggressive moves in the region, while making it seem as though Obama is standing up to the communists.

Before he arrived in Australia, Obama encouraged American business leaders to invest in communist China, telling them, "We should be rooting for China to grow." This statement was reported by Jackie Calmes of The New York Times, but not portrayed as a gaffe in any way.

Rather than being anti-China in any way, Obama's speech to the Australian Parliament was full of praise for the communist regime. He said, "…the United States will continue our effort to build a cooperative relationship with China. All of our nations—Australia, the United States—all of our nations have a profound interest in the rise of a peaceful and prosperous China. That's why the United States welcomes it."

The latter statement was the only perceived criticism of China, and it was extremely mild and non-specific. He said nothing about China's military build-up, including a new aircraft carrier, stealth jets, ICBMs, and cyber warfare, and its excessive territorial claims.

And media reports forgot to mention that Obama's statement that "We've seen that China can be a partner, from reducing tensions on the Korean Peninsula to preventing proliferation," was blatantly false.

On what basis does Obama claim that China is "a partner"

in "reducing tensions on the Korean Peninsula?"

In his speech, Obama mentioned North Korea's proliferation efforts but took China completely off the hook. Our media ignored this curious aspect of his performance.

He said, "...we also reiterate our resolve to act firmly against any proliferation activities by North Korea. The transfer of nuclear materials or material by North Korea to states or non-state entities would be considered a grave threat to the United States and our allies, and we would hold North Korea fully accountable for the consequences of such action."

There was no stated intention to hold China accountable.

Though it has a reputation for liberal bias, PBS's Ray Suarez was more accurate in discussing Obama's approach to China, saying that more than 2,000 American troops are heading to Australia under a new security agreement, but that Obama "stopped short of saying that the move is meant as a message to China."

Suarez went on to note that Obama "refused to make a direct link between Chinese actions and his announcement today."

Indeed, the 2,500 or so troops pose no threat to China. (Only 250 are scheduled to arrive next year and the rest would arrive by 2016.)

Australia is now faced with a country – China – which has nuclear weapons that can strike Australia, and this threat is growing. North Korea, assisted by China, is also developing nuclear weapons that could strike Australia.

But Obama does not want to single China out for criticism. Such an approach should make the U.S. and Australia nervous.

OLBERMANN AND LETTERMAN: MEN OF THE PEOPLE

By Roger Aronoff   October 25, 2011

Two extremely wealthy white American comedians, both who "earn" in excess of $10 million a year, gaggled recently on CBS's *The Late Show with David Letterman* about the "two or three percent of the people [who] have all the money" in this country, while expressing their solidarity with the Occupy Wall Street (OWS) movement.

I'm talking, of course, about David Letterman and Keith Olbermann.

The conversation started off with Letterman referring to Occupy Wall Street, saying, "I love this. I love people causing trouble…largely this is the only way we get change any more in this country. What do you know about the protesters?"

Olbermann replied:

"One of the big criticisms is that there's no set of demands. In other words, 'we want the Fed deregulated' [I believe he meant "regulated"], 'we want, we want something changed, we want more ice cream.' … They don't have a list of — on the premise that — few people are acknowledging that there's some sort of problem that needs to be investigated, and therefore, what they are saying is — nothing in the history of mankind has ever improved before somebody stood up and went 'this is screwed up, we need to fix this.' …So they're not, they're articulating, I think, a sense that we need to change this, and we need to be proactive about it because the country's for everybody, not just rich people."

Two or three percent "have all the money…," said Olbermann. Certainly these two clowns are in that two or three percent. They must be part of the problem, right?

Regarding a set of demands, perhaps Olbermann hasn't seen the 99% Declaration, representing a significant voice of the movement, that calls for, among other demands: "Elimination of the Corporate State...Elimination of Private Contributions to Politicians...Student Loan Forgiveness...Immigration Reform...End Outsourcing...Foreclosure Moratorium...Abolish the Electoral College... Ending the War in Afghanistan." There's something Keith can go investigate.

Olbermann said he went down to OWS in Lower Manhattan and walked through the crowd. Letterman said he'd be beaten if he went down there, but that he is "very sympathetic."

He said, "They don't like the idea that famous guys with dough are sucking up to them."

Their next target, of course, was Rush Limbaugh.

LETTERMAN:

"You know, here's something that is polarizing and was meant to be polarizing. Rush Limbaugh referred to those people down there as human debris. How can you be a human and call people who are uncertain and in some cases been left out, how can you call them debris?"

OLBERMANN:

"Well, I would consider the source on that, first off, because frankly, the man does know his human debris."

LETTERMAN:

"Well he had his house staff running to Guatemala to get painkillers. That's not human debris?"

Letterman goes after Rush for personal foibles. How does that compare to Letterman cheating on his wife by having sex with members of his staff?

PROGRESSIVE MEDIA ENCOURAGE LAWLESSNESS AND ANARCHY

By Cliff Kincaid   October 18, 2011

The anti-Wall Street demonstrators have taken over a private park in New York City and public property, Freedom Plaza and McPherson Square, in D.C. The reaction of the White House is that all of this is fine. After all, if you can take from the rich, why not take from the public.

The Republicans are now treating this lawlessness and anarchy as a serious and legitimate movement.

The website of the National Park Service says "Experience Your America," alluding to the fact that such places are supposed to be open to the public. But if you try to "experience" Freedom Plaza in Washington, D.C., which is under the jurisdiction of the Park Service, you will run into a filthy tent city in blatant violation of federal law forbidding tents and cooking facilities.

At the dedication of the Martin Luther King, Jr. memorial, Obama said, "If he were alive today, I believe he would remind us that the unemployed worker can rightly challenge the excesses of Wall Street without demonizing all who work there…" But the "unemployed" are not organizing these protests. I interviewed one organizer, Dennis Trainor, who has a job and makes a living doing videos of radical left activities around the country. A proponent of the view that capitalism is homicidal, he sees this as an opportunity to film the global revolution that they want to see unfold. Another organizer of the "October 2011" movement is Kevin Zeese, who once made a name for himself as a leader of the National Organization for the Reform of Marijuana Laws. He has reinvented himself as a "peace activist."

Another of the D.C. "Occupy" organizers, David Swanson, has a website devoted to his "writings" and wants people to believe he is a great thinker. His website is called "Let's try democracy," when in fact he is determined to take what is not his.

This movement is based on theft of other peoples' property. It fits perfectly into the Obama theme of taking from some to give to others.

What's more, the police, local and federal, are being told to ignore this lawlessness. The Washington Post reports that when the permit expired, the Park Police simply "issued an extension and amended the existing permit for the protesters at Freedom Plaza." In the McPherson Square area, the protesters never even obtained a permit to have a demonstration but were nevertheless "granted concessions" and the authorities "will not interfere as long as the campers are not a nuisance."

The fact that billionaire hedge fund operator George Soros, who is based in New York, has escaped the wrath of the protesters should tell us a lot. Needless to say, they won't be targeting Soros for sit-ins and other actions.

The situation is quickly getting out of control, thanks to President Obama, cowardly Republicans such as Eric Cantor, and media personalities such as Dylan Ratigan. A confrontation is inevitable because the protesters are refusing to move and the public is demanding access to the parks and public spaces they pay for.

OPERATION FAST AND FURIOUS: THE SCANDAL THAT CAN NO LONGER BE DENIED

By Roger Aronoff   September 29, 2011

The usual truism is that many politicians make the mistake of not coming completely clean when allegations of wrongdoing surface. The cover-up, it is said, is often worse than the underlying crime or ethical violation.

But in some cases, the crime, or lapse in judgment, is definitely worse than the cover-up. That appears to be the case in a simmering scandal engulfing the Obama administration that the mainstream media have tried their best to ignore for many months. It is known as Operation Fast and Furious.

It involves the Obama Justice Department and the Bureau of Alcohol, Tobacco and Firearms (ATF), as well as some 1,500 guns, about 1,000 of which ended up in Mexico, and a Border agent, Brian Terry, who was murdered with weapons found near the scene of the crime in Arizona. The weapons were among 57 linked to Fast and Furious that have been tied to at least 11 violent crimes in the U.S., including the Terry murder. The Justice Department, while largely stonewalling, has admitted this much to Congress, as reported by The Los Angeles Times.

There has been some good reporting on this issue by Sharyl Attkisson of CBS News, and Brian Ross of ABC News. Fox News has been all over the story, and Sean Hannity had a one-hour special back in July 2011 devoted to this emerging scandal. Others in the conservative media have done an excellent job, including Pajamas Media, Michelle Malkin, Andy McCarthy of National Review Online, American Thinker, WorldNetDaily, the Heritage Foundation and Andrew Breitbart through his many platforms, among others.

Even when the mainstream media have reported on this scandal, they have gone to great lengths to make sure that it didn't implicate President Obama, much less his Attorney General Eric Holder, for anything other than being out of the loop.

But that may have ended with recent revelations that the federal government apparently purchased weapons and sold them directly to criminals in Mexico. As Michael Walsh of the New York Post wrote, "the Department of Alcohol, Tobacco, Firearms and Explosives apparently ordered one of its own agents to purchase firearms with taxpayer money, and sell them directly to a Mexican drug cartel."

This revelation may prove to be the game changer, and force the Obama administration to turn this over to an independent counsel.

CNN has decided it can no longer duck and cover, and shield the Obama administration from a scandal that has the potential to make Whitewater and Watergate pale by comparison.

Anderson Cooper's reporter on this story, Drew Griffin, tried to explain a possible motive for Fast and Furious. "So what's the real purpose?" asked Griffin. "The lack of sense, the apparent cover-up has opened the door now for these conspiracy theorists. And you've got to follow this. They believe this was part of a convoluted plan for the Obama administration and the attorney general to actually increase the level of violence on the Mexican border with assault weapons purchased in the U.S. in an apparent attempt to rekindle interest in an assault weapons ban. "

MEDIA PREPARE RUSSIAN TREATY TRAP FOR THE U.S.

By Cliff Kincaid   August 30, 2011

"In a multinational race to seize the potential riches of the formerly icebound Arctic, being laid bare by global warming, Russia is the early favorite." So says the Christian Science Monitor. "At stake is an estimated one-quarter of all the world's untapped hydrocarbon reserves, abundant fisheries, and a freshly opened route that will cut nearly a third off the shipping time from Asia to Europe."

What the paper neglected to note is that the U.S. has exclusive rights to this region because Americans were the first to set foot on the North Pole. There is no Russian advantage, despite their planting a flag there in 2007. There is also a dispute, of course, about whether the "warming" is man-made or not.

"Within the next year," the paper went on, "the Kremlin is expected to make its claim to the United Nations in a bold move to annex about 380,000 square miles of the internationally owned Arctic to Russian control."

In fact, the Arctic is not "internationally owned" and the U.N. has no jurisdiction over the area unless and until the U.S. gives up its rights by ratifying the U.N.'s Law of the Sea Treaty.

As we have pointed out in the past, "American explorers staked an American claim to the North Pole in the early 1900s and U.S. nuclear submarines traveled below the Pole and broke the ice in the 1950s. Russian claims [to the region] are fraudulent and should be seen and rejected as such."

What makes this relevant and newsworthy is President Obama's push for ratification of the Law of the Sea Treaty, which would indeed put the region under the jurisdiction of global bureaucrats.

The Russians tried the same gambit under President Bush, who also pushed the treaty.

As long as the U.S. remains a non-party to the treaty, our rights are enforceable by the U.S. Navy. But once ratification takes place, we are at the mercy of foreign interests, including Russia and China, as well as international lawyers and bureaucrats.

The 202-page UNCLOS treaty document was described by the late leftist Senator Alan Cranston as "the most far-reaching and comprehensive system created thus far by the global community." UNCLOS mandates a global tax on corporations that exploit ocean resources, an International Seabed Authority to collect the revenue, and an International Tribunal on the Law of the Sea to govern ocean affairs.

Harvard law professor and international lawyer Louis B. Sohn, who himself advocated world government, was a key author of UNCLOS. He offered a detailed proposal to transform the United Nations into a world government in his book, *World Peace Through World Law*. He declared that he wanted this world government to maintain hundreds of thousands of troops, and military bases--and be armed with nuclear weapons. The purpose, he said, would be to disarm "each and every nation and to deter or suppress any attempted international violence."

This "world authority" would also require a "United Nations Revenue System," drawing taxes from "each nation" of the world, he said. UNCLOS was one of the steps in his scheme.

MEDIA'S DISGRACEFUL COVERAGE OF DEBT-CEILING DEBATE

By Roger Aronoff   July 29, 2011

Events are moving fast toward the artificial deadline of August 2nd, 2011. President Obama has apparently given up on getting a tax hike, and thus balance, as he has called it.

The general performance of the media during the debt ceiling debate has been atrocious.

The constant reference to August 2nd being the date we default on our debt is utterly false. ABC has shown a "Countdown to Default" clock, ticking away to August 2nd. CNN has run similar graphics, as have all the networks, including the Fox News Channel.

Default occurs only if, and when, the U.S. fails to make interest payments to the bondholders on the debt it owes. Not only is August 2nd not the day the U.S. defaults on its debt, but the issue could easily be taken off the table, and President Obama could calm the markets by announcing that under no circumstances will he allow the U.S. to default.

The other egregious falsehood reveals an astounding lack of knowledge, or willingness to deceive, about the difference between the deficit and the national debt. Here, for example, from Jake Tapper of ABC News: "The president continues to push for a 'grand bargain,' buoyed by the bipartisan 'Gang of Six' proposal that would reduce the deficit by $3.7 trillion over the next decade through spending cuts and tax increases."

As explained on the Treasury Department's own website, "The deficit is the difference between the money Government takes in, called receipts, and what the Government spends, called outlays, **each year**." (emphasis added) The same website says that "One way to think about the debt is as accumulated deficits."

But what they are really talking about is that under President Obama's ill-fated budget, as put forth in February, Obama projected spending of some $46 trillion over the next ten years. A $4 trillion cut means they would still be spending $42 trillion over that period. It's not a reduction of anything other than the stated, but unrealistic intentions of a ten-year budget with a four percent growth rate.

However, the size of the deficits each year is completely unpredictable and unknowable, and Congress is supposed to pass new budgets each year. In other words, this gives smoke and mirrors a bad name.

According to the Bipartisan Policy Institute, the payment of interest for the month of August would be $29 billion out of a monthly budget to run the U.S. Government of approximately $306 billion. It says that the U.S. Government will take in about $172 billion in August, enough to pay the interest on the debt, Social Security (which is technically in a separate trust fund), Medicare, Medicaid, Defense vendor payments and unemployment benefits.

To put these numbers in perspective, the first total U.S. annual budget to hit a $100 billion total was in the 1960s. Now, less than 50 years later, we have to borrow more than $135 billion *per month* to meet our obligations. So it is fair to say we have a spending problem.

ARE MIDWEST FLOODS CAUSED BY GLOBAL WARMING OR RADICAL ENVIRONMENTALISTS?

By Roger Aronoff   June 27, 2011

Many global warming alarmists are pointing to the floods in the Midwest as the latest proof of global warming. But a powerful piece at AmericanThinker.com provides an alternative suggestion as to the real cause of the flooding: the perhaps unintended consequences of radical environmentalist policies regarding the system of dams on the Missouri River.

Al Gore gave a speech in New York last week in which he linked the flooding in the Midwest and the fires in Arizona to global warming: "Today, the biggest fire in the history of the state of Arizona is spreading to New Mexico. Today, the biggest flood in the history of the Mississippi River Valley is under way right now," Gore said. "At what point is there a moment where we say, 'Oh, we ought to do something about this?'"

One of Gore's dimmer acolytes, Bill Maher, took up the issue on his show on HBO, "Real Time with Bill Maher." Maher seemed to be hooked up to a machine that gave him a shock every time he uttered the words "global warming," which he repeatedly did, before, in each case, correcting himself to say "climate change." Maher finally got it out, sort of, and asked, "Why doesn't he [Obama] point to this and say this is all because of climate change. He doesn't seem to use what he has to make a case."

But in the article, "The Purposeful Flooding of America's Heartland," in American Thinker, Joe Herring makes a very strong, well documented case, that the system of dams built in the area to tame the Missouri River and prevent this sort of thing from happening was well conceived and executed: "Some sixty years ago, the U.S. Army Corps of Engineers (USACE) began the process of taming the Missouri by constructing a series of six dams. The idea was simple: massive dams at the top moderating flow to the smaller dams below, generating electricity while providing desperately needed control of the river's devastating floods."

But in the 1990s the plan was hijacked by radical environmentalists with a different agenda: "The Clinton administration threw its support behind the change, officially shifting the priorities of the Missouri River dam system from flood control, facilitation of commercial traffic, and recreation to habitat restoration, wetlands preservation, and culturally sensitive and sustainable biodiversity."

Herring cites Greg Pavelka, a wildlife biologist with the Corps of Engineers in Yankton, SD, who told the Seattle Times that "this event will leave the river in a 'much more natural state than it has seen in decades,' describing the epic flooding as a 'prolonged headache for small towns and farmers along its path, but a boon for endangered species.'"

Herring also documents that, through a series of emails last February, "Ft. Pierre SD Director of Public Works Brad Lawrence sounded the alarm loud and clear," but the alarm of this "flood of biblical proportions" was not heeded. Why don't the mainstream media follow up on Mr. Herring's findings?

One organization that specializes in straight talk about global warming from actual scientists is The Heartland Institute, which sponsors conferences showing that evidence doesn't support the warming theory. According to Bob Carter, an Australian scientist who has participated in Heartland events, "Between 2001 and 2010 global average temperature decreased by 0.05 degrees, over the same time that atmospheric carbon dioxide levels increased by 5 per cent. Ergo, carbon dioxide emissions are not driving dangerous warming."

JUSTICE IN SHORT SUPPLY AT OBAMA'S DOJ

By Roger Aronoff   June 16, 2011

Attorney General Eric Holder has been under fire from the Left and the Right almost since taking office, but the mainstream media, at least until recently, have hardly taken note of why. The Obama Justice Department has been ideologically driven, politically correct, incompetent, and even corrupt, as they defy the courts and Congress alike.

While each emerging issue has received some coverage, rarely have any news stories focused on the systemic politicization and incompetence of the Obama Justice Department.

Michael Gerson, a former speechwriter for George W. Bush who became a Washington Post columnist, cited the handling of "the underwear bomber case." That was the incident on the plane from Europe to Detroit on Christmas Day, 2009, in which Umar Farouk Abdulmutallab planned to blow up the plane, but was thwarted.

The complaint in this case is that after a mere 50 minutes of interrogation, the terrorist suspect was read his Miranda rights. As Gerson put it, "Holder treated a national security judgment as a purely legal one."

The most high profile case is that of Khalid Sheikh Mohammed, the al-Qaeda member said to be, according to the 9/11 Commission Report, "the principal architect of the 9/11 attacks." In December of 2008, Khalid Sheikh Mohammed, along with four co-defendants, sent a letter to the judge of the military commission overseeing his case, expressing a desire to plead guilty.

But inexplicably, instead of accepting the confession, Attorney General Holder decided it would be better to try him in New York City, near the site of Ground Zero.

The list goes on. Andy McCarthy has been a persistent critic of Eric Holder on the pages of National Review.

He names several Islamist organizations in the U.S. that the Muslim Brotherhood has identified as its partners, including the Council on American Islamic Relations (CAIR), the Islamic Society of North America (ISNA), and the North American Islamic Trust (NAIT), all of which had been designated by prosecutors as "unindicted coconspirators" in the Holy Land Foundation case.

After the five indicted HLF defendants were convicted in 2008, the U.S. attorney in Dallas wanted to prosecute the unindicted co-conspirators. "They were thwarted, however," writes McCarthy, "by Obama political appointees at Main Justice" for "political considerations" having nothing to do with the evidence.

Another story that reflects badly on the Holder DOJ is "Project Gunrunner." It came to the public's attention when CBS News' Sharyl Attkisson reported that "Project Gunrunner" was having the effect of putting guns into the hands of Mexican drug traffickers," while intending to do exactly the opposite.

The idea was to stop the flow of weapons from the U.S. to Mexico's drug cartels. But in practice, ATF's actions had the opposite result: they allegedly facilitated the delivery of thousands of guns into criminal hands.

It is clear that the Department of Justice under Holder has become very politicized and has been drawn into the service of a left-wing, politically-correct agenda, and the media don't seem to care.

OBAMA ENERGY POLICIES RUNNING OUT OF GAS

By Roger Aronoff   May 6, 2011

One of the more important issues raised during the budget battle that nearly shut down the Federal government in April was over power given to the Environmental Protection Agency (EPA) by President Barack Obama to regulate greenhouse gases. This has led to renewed discussion on the validity of concerns about global warming, and the related issue of America's future energy sources.

In the mid 1970s, the big concern among so-called environmentalists was that we were heading toward a new Ice Age. The essence of that point of view was carried in a Newsweek article in April 28, 1975. They wrote, "The central fact is that after three quarters of a century of extraordinarily mild conditions, the earth's climate seems to be cooling down. Meteorologists disagree about the cause and extent of the cooling trend, as well as over its specific impact on local weather conditions."

It wasn't too long ago, 1988 to be specific, when that "almost unanimous" view shifted, and the problem had become catastrophic global warming. Larry Bell is a space architect and professor at the University of Houston, and author of the new book *Climate of Corruption: Politics and Power Behind the Global Warming Hoax*. In an interview in 2011 with AIM, Bell said that "Change is what climate does. It's measured, typically, in three-decade periods, although it didn't take three decades from the time of the '70s, when The New York Times and other organizations were reporting the next Ice Age coming, until Al Gore had his famous hearings in 1988, which declared not only that global warming was a crisis, but that we caused it."

The media were also complicit in pushing the global

warming hoax, calling skeptics "deniers," as in "Holocaust deniers." Newsweek used some form of the term "denier" 20 times in one 2007 cover story on global warming about those who don't buy into the theory.

A Scientific Consensus?

Thousands of advanced-degree scientists publicly refuted both the science and the fear mongering behind global warming, which has in recent years come to be known instead as climate change. It's an easier concept to sell, and it doesn't matter if the earth's temperature is rising or cooling, it is still climate change, and who can disagree with that?

What about the accusations that the skeptics were being financed by oil and industrial companies? When we wrote about this in 2007, those skeptical of global warming were estimated to have received tens of millions of dollars in funding, including some $19 million from ExxonMobil, but the other side – the side promoting global warming as an apocalyptic nightmare – had received some $50 billion. This figure, of course, doesn't include the dollar value of all of the media coverage in support of the theory.

Obama's ideologically driven energy policy is in tatters, and the media can't seem to help this time. It is time that he pursues a policy that will truly get America off of Middle Eastern oil, bolster the economy, and right the American ship of state.

ANDREW BREITBART'S RIGHTEOUS INDIGNATION: EXCLUSIVE INTERVIEW

By Roger Aronoff   May 5, 2011

Andrew Breitbart was a modern day media mogul. He created a series of websites that drew hundreds of thousands of people a day, sometimes millions a day, to see what he was up to now. And he made no bones about his politics and the journey from being a "default cultural liberal" to his current status as a "conservative culture warrior." He also considered himself to be a combatant in a battle of ideas and values against what he calls the "Democrat Media Complex."

With the release of his second book, *Righteous Indignation: Excuse Me While I Save the World*, Breitbart discussed his political journey, identified what's at stake and the other combatants in the current marketplace of ideas, and offered his ideas on how to overcome the built-in strengths of the complex.

I should also mention that he was the recipient of the 2010 Reed Irvine Award for his work in helping to uncover the scandal at ACORN.

Below, in italics, are excerpts from my interview with Andrew Breitbart. You can listen to the entire interview or read the transcript at www.aim.org.

Tom Brokaw — and Katie Couric-type people told me that Clarence Thomas was bad and Anita Hill was good. I saw that the National Organization for Women said that Clarence Thomas was bad and Anita Hill was good, so I was rooting for it. And I sat down and I watched the hearings, waiting for evidence that would prove the thesis—because he was ultimately on trial. By the end of the week, I thought to myself, When are they going to provide the evidence?...I saw that something was wrong here. That was my first epiphany. I didn't understand how the NAACP could sit back as these white, privileged men like Ted Kennedy—Ted Kennedy, the Ted Kennedy!—sat in judgment of another man as relates to his behavior around women. It just outraged me. But I didn't know what I was seeing.

I switched over to the AM dial, started listening to Rush Limbaugh, and, eventually, I started to come to grips with the fact that I may disagree with him politically, but he's not a racist. I wasn't hearing any of the type of stuff they had told me he was. But then I started to listen to him and Dennis Prager together, and I started to think to myself, 'Wait a second—these guys make so much more sense than all of my professors—excuse me—all of the celebrities in my life, all of my friends and family. These guys make more sense than anything I've ever heard in my entire life.'

I can go back to my history and say that the [Matt] Drudge thing was just pure luck. I met him at the very beginning. The first time I met him in person, he came over to Orson's house, when he was folding shirts at the CBS gift shop. He talked to me for four hours, and he left in his Hyundai, which putt-putted down the Venice Canal alleyway. I looked at my wife and I said, "That man's going to change the world. That guy is a media visionary." I knew it from the very, very beginning. That's definitely the smartest, most prescient moment of my life.

The Democratic Party, it's amazing. It gets away with murder with black people. They're the party of environmentalism, where "environmentalism" is defined-down to banning DDT from Africa, which has killed millions of people. The Democratic Party supports Planned Parenthood, created by Margaret Sanger, whose desire for eugenics was to limit the population of black people—and boy, has that been a success. The Great Society—welfare—has obliterated the family structure of the black community. I'm appalled by the Democratic Party as [it] relates to race. For these people, with their track record of enslaving black people, telling them they only have one point of view in this country, while, at the same time, destroying their communities, it's a crime against humanity—and I'm willing to fight. And if being called a racist for wanting to create a better society where black people have the freedom to think freely, if they want to call me a racist on national TV, I'm going to go there, and I'm going to fight back.

Hollywood is 100% controlled by the organized Left. And, it's through intimidation.

What the American people don't know—and look: Ideology matters more than money to these people. They're pretty good capitalists who mask their capitalism through an abrasive form of noblesse oblige liberalism. They're very good capitalists, but ideology means a lot to them, and they have a totalitarian instinct to punish those and to silence those who dissent. What I've discovered in recent years is that there is a silent group of people—thousands strong, perhaps tens of thousands strong—who silently languish in the industry. Actors, directors, writers, below-the-line people, producers, agents, heads of studios who happen to be conservative or libertarian, but are secretive about it because the institutional Left will punish them—and there's plausible-deniability-blacklisting that goes on in Hollywood.

This book is, basically, a how-to-manual. Once you see how I went from a default cultural liberal to being a culture warrior for the Right, I think your eyes will be opened as to how bad the problem is. I provide the tactics that you can use to fight the battle against the Democrat Media Complex. I don't think that the next election cycle's about beating Barack Obama—I think Barack Obama has already lost. The next election cycle is against the mainstream media, who's going to try and carry his political corpse over the finish line. So the way to win in 2012 is to expose the truth about Barack Obama, not to be afraid of the Democrat Media Complex calling you names—and to just fight, fight, fight! And Righteous Indignation, *which is available at Breitbartbook.com, will show you how you can wield new media and have a, great, great effect in electoral politics.*

BIN LADEN IS DEAD BUT HIS NETWORK LIVES

By Cliff Kincaid   May 3, 2011

Al-Jazeera's obituary of Osama bin Laden, the founder of al Qaeda, calls him the man "allegedly" behind the terrorist attacks of September 11, 2001. This odd formulation reflects the channel's favorable coverage of the 9/11 "truth" movement, which pinned the attacks on the U.S. and/or Israeli governments. But even more significant is the fact that Al-Jazeera was bin Laden's medium of choice and transmitted his anti-American message to millions of Arabs and Muslims. This is a fact that the network does not want to trumpet.

Many of the video and audio recordings released by Osama bin Laden were apparently transmitted by courier to Al-Jazeera. One Al-Jazeera correspondent, Tayseer Alouni, went to prison in Spain after being convicted of being a courier for al Qaeda. Another Al-Jazeera employee, Sami al-Hajj, was imprisoned at Guantanamo Bay and released. However, his military file includes allegations that that he was a courier for al Qaeda as well.

This is significant because of the reports that bin Laden was tracked down through one of his couriers.

For its part, the channel declares, "Thousands of lives have been lost in several countries in what the US calls its 'war on terror'—from Afghanistan and Pakistan to Iraq and London, where civilians bore the brunt of attacks and retaliatory attacks." Notice how the U.S. is blamed for taking the fight to the terrorists targeting Americans for death. This is vintage Al-Jazeera. The channel continues to be scrutinized for its curious coverage of major news events that put aspects of the Arab/Muslim world in a negative light.

Trying to explain why Al-Jazeera English didn't devote a story to the assault on CBS News correspondent Lara Logan, the channel's Al Anstey was quoted as saying that they "couldn't cover everyone that was hurt" during the riots in Egypt. The more logical explanation is that Al-Jazeera had an agenda, and covering the attack on Logan might have undermined the notion that the demonstrators were pro-democracy fighters.

The notion that Logan was only "hurt" is a further insult to the reporter, who has now spoken publicly about the sexual assault.

In advance of her Sunday "60 Minutes" appearance to talk about the rape by 200 Egyptian men, CBS News reported that "Logan lost contact with her colleagues for approximately 25 minutes and endured a sexual assault and beating that she feared she would not survive."

On "60 Minutes," she said, "They literally tore my pants to shreds. And then I felt my underwear go." She broke down in tears as she described being raped with their hands, leaving her with internal injuries, while other members of the mob tried to pull off her arms. Egyptian soldiers saved her in the end, but she was in the hospital for four days.

"It's not likely anyone involved will be brought to justice," said CBS News correspondent Scott Pelley, who interviewed Logan.

Al-Jazeera has shown no desire to bring the rapists of Lara Logan to justice, but it is demanding information on one of its own journalists missing in Syria.

FORMER AL-JAZEERA AND NPR REPORTER NOW WORKING FOR CASTRO

By Cliff Kincaid   April 13, 2011

He used to be a correspondent for Al-Jazeera English in Communist Cuba, reporting "objectively" on what is happening in Castro's island paradise. Now, Juan Jacomino is the Second Secretary of the Cuban Interests Section in Washington, D.C., where he is coordinating "solidarity" activities for the regime.

His transition from Al-Jazeera to official Castro mouthpiece and "diplomat" demonstrates that the news channel has extremely low standards for deciding who is fit to be a "journalist." It is another major embarrassment for Al-Jazeera, which wants to be taken seriously as a professional news organization.

But that's not all. It turns out that Jacomino also worked for a news agency that supplied news and information to CBS News, National Public Radio and Fox News Radio in the U.S.

The Cuban Interests Section, featured on Jacomino's business card, is considered Castro's embassy in Washington, D.C., since the U.S and Cuba do not have diplomatic relations. But it is known to be a nest of spies for Castro.

It turns out that Jacomino, who has his own Facebook page, worked for the Cuban government before he became a correspondent for Al-Jazeera. Back in 1997, during an on-line discussion of a U.S. academic trip to Cuba, Jacomino was described as "a journalist at Radio Havana Cuba who specializes in the economy and was previously a functionary at the Foreign Ministry." This trip was arranged at the time by the pro-Castro group Global Exchange, headed by Medea Benjamin of Code

Pink. Typically, these visits are designed to expose American academics and journalists to propaganda from communist officials.

Radio Havana Cuba is the official government-run international broadcasting station of Cuba.

Jacomino has apparently "returned" to official government employment, a topic I raised when I came upon Jacomino and got his business card while covering the Latin American Solidarity Coalition conference in Washington, D.C. Jacomino assured me that Cuba's recent decision to fire hundreds of thousands of government workers did not mean the regime was going capitalist.

Jacomino has also worked for Global Radio News, which describes itself as a network of freelance reporters. Here is where it gets real interesting. The list of GRN clients includes Al-Jazeera, ABC Australia, BBC World Service, Canadian Broadcasting Corporation, CBS, CBS News, CBS Radio, Fox News Radio, Fox TV, ITN, National Public Radio, Russia Today, Radio Live New Zealand, Sirius Radio, and Sky News, among others.

While Jacomino has left Al-Jazeera, the anti-American bias will remain. Consider this one-sided Al-Jazeera story featuring Gloria La Riva of the "National Committee to Free the Cuban Five." La Riva, an official of the U.S.-based communist group known as the Party for Socialism and Liberation, was considered an objective source by the "news" channel and no other view was presented.

The fact that an agent of Castro wormed his way into the channel and became a source for a news agency supplying American news organizations with information from around the world is alarming. But don't look for any investigations by the media into how they were duped by a mouthpiece for the Castro regime.

AMERICAN JOURNALISTS RUB ELBOWS WITH TERROR-FRIENDLY MIDDLE EAST DICTATORSHIP

By Cliff Kincaid   April 12, 2011

Media figures David Gregory of NBC's "Meet the Press," David Brooks of The New York Times, Fareed Zakaria of CNN's "GPS," Margaret Warner of PBS's "Newshour," and Riz Khan of Al-Jazeera English are among the speakers at the eighth Annual U.S.-Islamic World Forum in Washington, D.C. this week. The event is "held in partnership" with Qatar, the Middle East dictatorship that funds and sponsors the terror channel Al-Jazeera and has links to al-Qaeda.

The forum is co-sponsored by the liberal Brookings Institution, headed by former Clinton State Department official Strobe Talbott. Secretary of State Hillary Clinton is a speaker.

The official program guide for the conference features greetings from President Obama. "I appreciate your efforts to help advance the new beginning I called for between the United States and Muslim communities around the world," he says.

However, the 9/11 commission demonstrated that Qatar has been protecting terrorists, including the mastermind of 9/11, Khalid Sheikh Mohammed. A recently released cable from WikiLeaks goes further, saying that Qatari nationals were involved in 9/11 and may still be on the loose.

Meantime, Sultan al-Khalaifi, who is a Qatari blogger and the founder of a human rights organization, was apprehended on March 1 by Qatar's dreaded security forces and has not been heard of since. Human rights organizations fear that he is being tortured for speaking out against the dictatorship in Qatar.

At a recent press conference, under the auspices of the forum, two academics from the University of Maryland admitted they didn't know anything about the plight of the blogger.

The U.S.-Islamic Forum also features Muslim Democrat Representative Bruce Ellison, a vocal opponent of recent congressional hearings into the radicalization of Muslims in the U.S., and representatives of such groups as the Islamic Society of North America and the Muslim American Society. Officials of the repressive Qatari government are sprinkled on various panels throughout the three-day conference.

While Secretary of State Clinton is speaking to the conference and treating Qatar as a friend, secret cables released by WikiLeaks demonstrate that officials of the State Department do not regard the regime as helping the U.S. in the war on terrorist groups such as al-Qaeda.

One cable says that the regime has "adopted a largely passive approach to cooperating with the U.S. against terrorist financing" and that terrorist groups such as al-Qaeda "exploit Qatar as a fundraising locale." The cable goes on, "Although Qatar's security services have the capability to deal with direct threats and occasionally have put that capability to use, they have been hesitant to act against known terrorists out of concern for appearing to be aligned with the U.S. and provoking reprisals."

Another cable says that "Qatar will continue to use Al Jazeera as a bargaining tool to repair relationships with other countries, particularly those soured by Al Jazeera's broadcasts, including the United States." It also says, "Anecdotal evidence suggests, and former Al Jazeera board members have affirmed, that the United States has been portrayed more positively since the advent of the Obama administration."

OBAMA DECONSTRUCTED: AN INTERVIEW WITH JACK CASHILL

By Roger Aronoff   March 28, 2011

In an exclusive interview with Accuracy in Media, journalist and author Jack Cashill recently discussed his new book, *Deconstructing Obama: The Life, Loves and Letters of America's First Postmodern President*. In it, Cashill makes a convincing case that Obama did not write the two books that helped launch his candidacy: *Dreams from My Father* and *The Audacity of Hope*. He argues that *Dreams* was actually written by William Ayers, the unrepentant terrorist who was a founder of the communist Weather Underground.

By comparing Obama's book to Ayers' book, *Fugitive Days: A Memoir*, Cashill finds examples of the same unlikely spelling errors in each, a number of the same listed literary influences, and similar qualities and features in the writing that are understandable for Ayers, but not likely at all – according to Cashill's analysis – for Obama.

Even Obama's supporters on the Left have called for him to release his birth certificate, because they assume there is nothing to hide. Chris Matthews, David Corn and Clarence Page all urged Obama to do so, because, as Corn, the Washington bureau chief for Mother Jones magazine, said, "then we can make even more fun of the birthers."

Back on December 27th of 2010, on MSNBC's Hardball with Chris Matthews, the three of them rather reluctantly joined the chorus, but they did so nonetheless.

With more than 10 states in the process of attempting to pass laws requiring presidential candidates to release their birth certificates in order to be on the ballot in those states, even in 2012 in most cases, the subject takes on added importance.

Besides these issues, we talked about the downing of TWA Flight 800, about which we both produced documentaries looking into what happened back in 1996, when that plane exploded over the Atlantic, killing all 230 aboard. We both, after extensive research and interviewing eyewitnesses and experts, and reviewing the available evidence, are convinced that the plane was brought down by missiles.

Below, in italics, are excerpts from my interview with Cashill.

Iran doesn't guard its nuclear secrets as tightly as he guards his birth certificate. What's this all about? What kind of crazy thing is this? Why do we even have to ask? Why didn't the media ask these questions two, three years ago when they could have—and should have? Why didn't our media—the conservative media—raise these questions?

…if I'm right, not only is Obama not a genius, but he's a liar of some consequence. He disowned Ayers—he barely knew this guy, "a guy in the neighborhood"—and not only that, but he had allowed this guy, a self-proclaimed Communist, to crawl around inside of his head for a mind meld of some proportion that we did not want to happen in our White House—because, even now, Ayers has extortionate power over Barack Obama.

But when you're watching this in the campaign, and you're onto this story, you're saying, "Why isn't anyone in the major media asking how it is that this radical anti-Semite, Khalid al Mansour, was pushing Obama into Harvard twenty years before the election?" Isn't this worth investigating, this connection? No it wasn't—it was worth burying…But they just buried that whole story, and when I saw that—I mean, you know this, and you and Accuracy Media have been confronting this for years, how they bury stories that they simply don't want to share with the rest of the world.

…but at the end of the day—and I've looked at Obama's life very carefully—I think what's underestimated about Obama— and it tempers his radicalism—is his ambition. He is ambitious. He uses people. He's used them all his life. I think he was using al-Mansour, rather than the other way around. I think he was using Bill Ayers. I mean, Bill Ayers was trying to use him too, but the calculation that went into Dreams from My Father *in 1995 wasn't to elect the President of the United States, it was to elect the Mayor of Chicago. As Mayor, Obama could do Ayers a world of good, because Ayers was a power broker in Chicago, a big educational honcho. The same year the book came out, '95, Ayers had appointed Obama chairman of the $150 million slush fund called the Chicago Annenberg Challenge. He launched his campaign that year, with a fundraiser from Ayers' house. Yeah, Obama was Ayers' protégé…The guy is steely and ambitious— and do not underestimate that ambition.*

There's unintended humor here. This is David Axelrod. He's very close to the camp—he's the campaign's main strategist. It's not like he was just some clown who didn't know better. When Politico comes to him—and Politico's a very influential inside-the-Beltway publication, allegedly centrist, but not, it obviously skews Left—and asked him about whether they (Obama and Ayers) knew each other, Axelrod said, "Yeah, their kids went to school together. That was their only contact." Now, Ben Smith, who's writing about this for Politico, later, under pressure from his readers, adds what he calls an "update." It should have been labeled "Humiliated Correction." Because when Obama's oldest daughter starts kindergarten, Bill Ayers's youngest child is 23 years old.

There's a ruthless quality about the guy, by the way. Keep that in mind. And then he had to write The Audacity of Hope. *Now, it's sort of a memoir, kind of a policy brief that came out about two years later. David Remnick, the New Yorker editor, Pulitzer Prize winner, and a chief Obama biographer, tells us that, yeah, he wrote a chapter a weekend because he fell behind. The chapters are 50 pages long. Obama can't write. This book is an entirely different style than* Dreams from My Father. *It's clearly written by a different author...The chief suspect—I would say the only real good suspect—is Jon Favreau, his young speechwriter, who has written most of his famous speeches, starting back to 2004.*

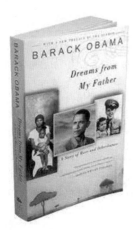

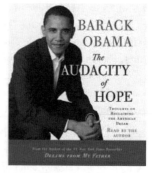

DID MUSLIM LOBBY FORCE FIRING OF POPULAR RADIO HOST?

By Cliff Kincaid   March 3, 2011

Washington, D.C. radio station WMAL is once again being accused of firing a popular talk show host because of his criticism of radical Muslims. The station, a major source of news and information for the nation's capital, claims that popular morning host Fred Grandy resigned on his own, but Grandy tells AIM that he was essentially forced to leave after his wife, who is also outspoken about radical Islam, was cut from the program.

The growing controversy over Grandy's departure has resulted in some Grandy supporters charging the station with being "Sharia-compliant," and with bending under pressure from the Council on American Islamic-Relations (CAIR), a Muslim lobbying organization that combats what it calls "Islamophobia" in the media.

Grandy, a former actor and Republican member of Congress, told AIM, "My wife and I have used our program over the last several months to warn about the spread of radical Islam at home and abroad. Last week, Catherine (known on the show as Mrs. Fred) delivered a very tough indictment against stealth jihad, and for her efforts she was told she was off the show. I then told management without Mrs. Fred at the microphone, I could not remain either and have resigned effective this morning."

A WMAL statement, which makes no mention of terminating "Mrs. Fred," was released on Thursday and claimed, "Fred Grandy has informed WMAL of his intention to resign from the station and its morning program, The Grandy Group. Veteran broadcast talent Bryan Nehman will continue to anchor the morning program and in the interim will be joined by several notable guest hosts and regular contributors. ....WMAL remains committed to its goal of providing a forum for discussing a broad spectrum of issues while delivering compelling programming including Chris Plante, Rush Limbaugh, Sean Hannity, and Mark Levin."

The statement on the Grandy matter was read on the air by another WMAL host, Chris Plante, who said that his broadcast opposition to radical Islam has not been curtailed in any way.

Grandy told AIM, "We cannot affirmatively conclude CAIR or any of the prominent Islamic organizations had anything to do with this. We do know, however, in 2005 representatives of CAIR in D.C. were successful in getting midmorning host Michael Graham fired for anti-Islamic statements he had made on the radio and TV."

Graham was fired from WMAL after describing Islam as a "terrorist organization" on his program and refusing to apologize or modify the description.

CAIR Communications Director Ibrahim Hooper acted surprised by the news of Grandy's resignation and responded, "What is their evidence for that claim?," when informed that his group was being blamed for his departure.

James Lafferty of the Virginia Anti-Shariah Task Force told AIM, "I heard from two very good sources that CAIR was involved in this and not only targeting Grandy but Sean Hannity." He said CAIR's strategy was to knock Grandy off the air and then go after Hannity, a nationally syndicated radio host carried by WMAL in the afternoon.

NBC'S MITCHELL REGURGITATES GADDAFI LIES

By Cliff Kincaid   February 22, 2011

The old lie about Libyan dictator Muammar Gaddafi's daughter supposedly being killed in a 1986 raid ordered by then-President Reagan is back. Several stories in U.S. and foreign media about the turmoil in Libya have discussed Gaddafi's rule in Libya, involvement in terrorism, and the time when we had a President, Ronald Reagan, who ordered military retaliation against pro-terrorist dictators.

On Monday's NBC Nightly News, reporter Andrea Mitchell said Libya was "accused of bombing a Berlin nightclub frequented by U.S. soldiers" and that "Ronald Reagan retaliated, ordering an air strike against Gaddafi's tent, accidentally killing his young daughter. Gaddafi escaped unharmed."

Mitchell had also flashed a photo of Gaddafi standing next to a girl—the "daughter"—who looked about six or seven years old.

It appears that Gaddafi "adopted" the girl after the strike in order to generate sympathy for himself. Mitchell omitted the "adopted" part.

Making Reagan out to be a heartless brute, Mitchell showed Reagan justifying the attack on Libya by saying, "if necessary we will do it again."

Contrary to Mitchell's claim about Libyan involvement in the nightclub bombing being just an accusation, John Koehler's book, *Stasi: The Untold Story of the East German Secret Police,* documents the Libyan role--with East German support--in the La Belle bombing in Berlin in April of 1986. Koehler says the East Germans were operating with the knowledge and approval of the Soviet intelligence service, the KGB.

Mitchell also neglected to note that the bombing killed two Americans and a Turkish woman, and injured well over 200 persons, including 41 Americans.

But the alleged death of Gaddafi's "daughter" was the worst part of the broadcast. The fact that stories about this alleged dead daughter are still appearing this many years later shows how easy it is to fool the major media.

Former USA Today reporter Barbara Slavin, who was in Libya at the time, set the record straight. "His adopted daughter was not killed," she told me. "An infant girl was killed. I actually saw her body. She was adopted posthumously by Gaddhafi. She was not related to Gadhafi."

On Monday night, CBS Evening News correspondent Mark Phillips said that Reagan's raid on Libya "killed about 60 people, including Gaddafi's 15-month-old adopted daughter."

Time magazine claimed Reagan's strike "killed 41 people including Gaddafi's adopted daughter."

ABC News claimed the victim was his "adopted baby daughter."

In a profile of Gaddafi, Al-Jazeera reported that "Libya's alleged involvement in the 1986 bombing of a Berlin nightclub in which two American soldiers were killed prompted U.S. air attacks on Tripoli and Benghazi, killing 35 Libyans, including Gaddafi's adopted daughter."

So the death toll is anywhere from 35 to 60. The media don't know--and don't seem to care--whether they get it right or wrong.

We can be sure that resurrecting these allegations in this case gave the media the opportunity to bash Ronald Reagan while discussing Gaddafi's tenuous hold on power.

NBC'S DAVID GREGORY WORRIES ABOUT LEGITIMACY OF OBAMA PRESIDENCY

By Cliff Kincaid   February 14, 2011

NBC's "Meet the Press" Host David Gregory berated House Speaker John Boehner (R-OH) because members of the public and the Congress have doubts about President Obama's professed Christian faith and alleged birth in the United States. Gregory wondered if all the doubts about Obama were undermining his legitimacy as President. He wanted Boehner to denounce these questions and concerns as "ignorance." Boehner refused to do so.

In fact, as AIM has noted, calling yourself something is not the same thing as proving it is the case. Obama's Christian claim deserves to be scrutinized, even when it involves a sensitive and personal matter such as religious belief. Our media are supposed to question the statements of those in power.

The facts show that there is no evidence that Obama was baptized in a traditional Christian sense of the term. Indeed, Muslims could join the church in Chicago that Obama attended.

Boehner said that it wasn't his job "to tell the American people what to think" and that he accepts the President's claim that he is a Christian. Gregory said such a response was playing "fast and loose" with the "obvious facts." Boehner replied, "I just outlined the facts as I understand them. I believe that the President is a citizen. I believe the President is a Christian. I'll take him at his word."

Here are the facts, from Obama's own perspective. Obama acknowledges in his autobiography *Dreams from My Father* that his grandfather was a Muslim and that he spent two years in a Muslim school in Indonesia studying the Koran. In *The Audacity of Hope*, he says that "my father had been raised a Muslim," but that by the time he met his mother, his father was a "confirmed atheist." His stepfather was not particularly religious and his mother professed "secularism," Obama wrote, but as a child he went to a "predominantly Muslim school," after being first sent to a Catholic school. His mother, he said, was concerned about him learning math, not religion.

Refusing to provide the facts about Obama's Muslim upbringing to his audience, Gregory moved on to the birth certificate issue.

He was particularly concerned that "a new tea party freshman who was out just yesterday speaking to conservatives...said, 'I'm fortunate enough to be an American citizen by birth, and I do have a birth certificate to prove it.'"

He wanted to know why Boehner isn't standing up to "misinformation" and "stereotypes."

With this comment, Gregory proved not only that he is a sycophant for Obama, but that he doesn't have a sense of humor. Raul Labrador's cited comments to the 2011 Conservative Political Action Conference (CPAC) were obviously in jest, although he was making a serious point. Pro-Obama journalists have consistently ignored questions about the constitutional eligibility of the current occupant of the oval office.

Our media should be performing that function, but they refuse to do so. They have simply accepted a vague "certification of live birth" from the Obama campaign as legitimate.

David Gregory is the ignorant one.

MEDIA PLAYING CRUCIAL ROLE IN MIDDLE EAST UPRISINGS

By Roger Aronoff   February 9, 2011

The events unfolding in Egypt that began on January 25, 2011 were indeed historic, but they may well be obscuring a much bigger story going on in the region, that has been generally ignored by the mainstream press.

Many of the anchors and correspondents from the major networks dutifully made the trek to Cairo to bear witness to the demonstrations: Katie Couric, Brian Williams, Anderson Cooper, and Christiane Amanpour. But while reporting with the crowds in the background, were they really able to glean what was going on?

The Muslim Brotherhood came late to the protests, we were told, but don't worry, there is nothing to fear from them. After all, they make up no more than 30 percent of the population. However, with no other groups well organized, besides the military, 30 percent makes the Brotherhood the political power center inside Egypt.

Richard Engel, of NBC News, said of the Muslim Brotherhood that "A lot of them are truly patriotic Egyptians," and that "They were nice people. I mean, if you fell down in the street, they would come and help you out." But he offered this warning, whether intentional or not: "They control a lot of the organizations that people would think are popular, a lot of the labor unions, the lawyers union, the different professional syndicates in this country."

I've watched hours of Al-Jazeera during the past couple of weeks, and they don't seem concerned about the inclusion of the Muslim Brotherhood at all. As AIM's Cliff Kincaid pointed out in a recent column, "Al-Jazeera consistently and misleadingly describes the Muslim Brotherhood as a 'non-violent' organization. In return, the Muslim Brotherhood describes Al-Jazeera as 'the greatest Arab media organization.'"

Of the despots, monarchs, theocrats and tyrants that operate in the Middle East, from an American national security perspective, Egypt has been a relatively reliable ally, in terms of maintaining peace with Israel, and not supporting groups such as Hamas in Gaza. Frankly it would have been preferable for other governments, most notably Iran, to fall to democratic revolutions before Egypt.

Maybe in the next presidential election, we will be debating "who lost Egypt."

Democracy is more than just holding one election. It is the establishment of a free press, an independent judiciary, freedom of association, and multiple elections, followed by a peaceful transfer of power. In other words, it doesn't happen overnight.

Many in the media have been assuring us that the Muslim Brotherhood is no longer a problem. "Very moderate," said Peter Bergen on MSNBC's Hardball. An article on CNN's website said that they've "long ago renounced violence as a means to achieve their domestic agenda of Islamic change."

For now the question is, can and should the Muslim Brotherhood be welcomed, or allowed in as part of the new regime that will replace Hosni Mubarak sometime later this year?

The question of whether or not this democratic uprising will successfully overturn historical precedent and withstand the hijacking by radicals that normally occurs in this part of the world is yet to be answered.

FOUL PLAY OR "FAIR GAME?"

By Roger Aronoff   February 7, 2011

By now the movie version of the Valerie Plame book, *Fair Game*, has been so thoroughly debunked, as has the version of history that it purports to tell, that it hardly seems necessary to go back down this path again. Although the movie bombed at the box office, its assault on the truth will continue on as a DVD release, video-on-demand, premium cable and on network TV.

The three basic lies of the story the makers and actors tell are these: 1) The Bush administration knowingly lied us into war against Saddam Hussein's Iraq by twisting evidence to make people believe there were weapons of mass destruction (WMD); 2) when former ambassador Wilson blew the whistle on Bush and Cheney for doing so, they got back at him by outing his wife, a covert CIA agent; and 3) Scooter Libby led the White House effort to out Ms. Plame and discredit her husband, and then took the fall for the administration. Within these lies are a whole series of lies and misrepresentations and deliberate damage done to the reputations of a lot of people.

The New York Times, in its review of the film, acknowledges that the film does "not disguise its sympathies."

Surprisingly, The Washington Post has been among Wilson's harshest critics. In a December 3 editorial, they wrote, "'Fair Game,' based on books by Mr. Wilson and his wife, is full of distortions—not to mention outright inventions." They added that "Hollywood has a habit of making movies about historical events without regard for the truth; 'Fair Game' is just one more example." We couldn't have said it better ourselves.

What else shows the dishonesty of the film? In some cases, it is what was left out. For instance, there was no reference to George Tenet's statement, released on July 11, between the release of Wilson's column on July 6, 2003, and Novak's on July 14 (though Novak's column was actually in newsrooms on July 11, which could go a long way toward explaining how many news people became aware of Plame's identity).

As Stan Crock pointed out in his article for the World Affairs Journal, "Valerie Plame says in her memoir that she read the report that the CIA wrote immediately after debriefing Wilson on his trip and also read his column before it was published. She added that she thought the column was accurate. She said the report was only a few pages long. No one, let alone a professional intelligence officer, could have missed the part about Iraq trying to buy yellowcake. …she was anything but an innocent bystander as her husband created a political firestorm."

In short, Libby was convicted of a motiveless crime for which there was no direct evidence, only the jury's unscientific inference of wrongdoing based on evidence that America's leading memory expert describes as completely inadequate to a reasoned judgment. If Hollywood wanted to make a fair film about a great injustice, that would have been the place to start.

OBAMA BOWS TO CASTRO

By Cliff Kincaid   January 17, 2011

On a recent "Meet the Press," host David Gregory tried to use the Arizona tragedy in which Jared Loughner shot and killed six people and wounded 12 others, including Rep. Gabrielle Giffords (D-AZ), to browbeat Republicans into stopping their tough criticism of President Obama's agenda. Gregory said, "you know as well as I do that there are people—and it is true that it's very often on the right—who describe President Obama as somehow an outsider who's trying to usher in a system that will do two things, that will injure America and deny them of their liberty. Do you condemn that belief…?"

Gregory failed to note that, two days earlier, Obama bolstered the communist dictatorship in Cuba.

The New York Times noted that the White House lifted restrictions on travel and payments to communist Cuba "when most Republican members of Congress were away on retreat and Democrats had left their offices for the long holiday weekend," and that the timing "indicated that the administration hoped to enact the changes with as little fanfare—and backlash—as possible." The changes were posted at 5:42 p.m. EST on Friday.

Another point, not mentioned, was that the nation was supposed to be in mourning over the Arizona massacre. But Obama used this as an opportunity, in the words of Democratic Senator Robert Menendez (D-NJ), to "extend an economic life line to the Castro regime."

Politico reported that the pro-Castro ruling "was delayed until after the midterms at the request of some Florida Democrats who feared blowback from their Cuban-American constituents."

To make matters worse, the Obama White House extended a helping hand to the communist regime at a time when American Alan Gross has been in prison in Cuba without charges for more than a year. Gross was working on a U.S. foreign aid project to help ordinary Cubans communicate with the outside world.

He has lost 90 pounds in captivity and is losing feeling in his right foot.

No wonder the Obama Administration carried out this despicable policy change when it thought few people would be paying attention. The Obama position is one of hope that Gross will eventually be released, after being tried in a kangaroo court, while the Castro regime benefits from more cash flowing into the communist-controlled island.

The White House timing and ploy worked. The major media ignored or played down Obama's bow to the Castro brothers. The Times story was carried on page five; The Washington Post ran a story about this back on page nine.

Not only has nothing changed for the better, in terms of human rights in Cuba, but an American continues to be held without charges.

In addition, the Castro dictatorship harbors American terrorists such as Joanne Chesimard, who escaped from a prison in the U.S. with the help of the Weather Underground after being convicted of murdering a New Jersey State Trooper.

Republican Senator Marco Rubio declared, "It is unthinkable that the administration would enable the enrichment of a Cuban regime that routinely violates the basic human rights and dignity of its people."

MEDIA EXCUSE OBAMA'S LIES ABOUT SHOOTINGS

By Cliff Kincaid   January 13, 2011

The liberal media have gone from blaming conservatives for the Arizona shootings to praising President Obama's speech, in which he made the false claim that nobody knows why the massacre happened. "For the truth is none of us can know exactly what triggered this vicious attack," Obama said. "None of us can know with any certainty what might have stopped these shots from being fired, or what thoughts lurked in the inner recesses of a violent man's mind."

In fact, all of the available evidence indicates that Jared Loughner is psychotic, and that his documented use of marijuana and other mind-altering drugs may have triggered his psychosis.

Obama, a former marijuana user, may not want to acknowledge this fact because his administration is soft on drugs and even buys into the "medical marijuana" scam. In 2004, Obama favored decriminalization of marijuana. As President, his Attorney General Eric Holder has withdrawn some federal resources from the war on drugs.

James Watson, the co-discoverer of DNA, linked marijuana and schizophrenia in 2010 in an interview, saying, "It's clear that if you're pre-disposed to schizophrenia, smoking marijuana will tip you over. But marijuana won't tip over someone into schizophrenia that is probably not predisposed to it."

In addition to the scholarly work, "Marijuana and Madness," the *British Journal of Psychiatry* published a study, "High-potency cannabis and the risk of psychosis," which concluded that "people with a first episode of psychosis had smoked higher-potency cannabis, for longer and with greater frequency, than a healthy control group…"

Nasser Rey, a friend of Loughner's from elementary and middle school, is quoted in The Washington Post as saying that, after high school, Loughner talked a lot about smoking marijuana and taking mushrooms.

This adds to the abundant evidence from public reports, detailed in my previous column, that Loughner's curious behavior was related to the heavy use of marijuana and other dangerous drugs.

Writing at the American Thinker, Jan LaRue, senior legal analyst with the American Civil Rights Union, noted, "Mental health experts have opined that Loughner's threatening and bizarre behavior, his videos, and nonsensical writings are consistent with a history of heavy marijuana use. The facts indicate that Loughner preferred a pot party to a tea party."

Some in the liberal media may be coming around to reality. Time magazine's Joe Klein acknowledges the possibility that Loughner "was a paranoid schizophrenic whose illness was exacerbated by frequent marijuana use."

He doesn't seem to want to acknowledge the complete truth because he has been a supporter of marijuana legalization.

In the past, Charles Lane of The Washington Post had noted that "the legalization of physician-recommended pot in California is a prescription for disaster…"

Ominously, on November 2, 2010, Arizona legalized "medical marijuana," to be dispensed by the state, by passing Proposition 203. A fact sheet from the Drug Enforcement Administration, one part of the federal government still run by a holdover from the Bush Administration, identified George Soros as one of the major funders of the initiative.